The Atonement and Modern Thought

BY

REV. JUNIUS B. REMENSNYDER, D. D., LL. D.,

Author of "Heavenward," "Doom Eternal," "Six Days of
Creation," "Lutheran Manual," etc., etc.

WITH AN INTRODUCTION
BY
PROF. BENJAMIN B. WARFIELD, D. D., LL. D.,

OF PRINCETON THEOLOGICAL SEMINARY

*"The death of Christ is the crown of His redemptive
work."*–IRENÆUS

THE ATONEMENT AND MODERN THOUGHT
By Junius Benjamin Remensnyder

Just & Sinner
425 East Lincoln Ave.
Watseka, IL 60970

www.JustandSinnerPublishing.com

ISBN 10: 0692627162
ISBN 13: 978-0692627167

ORIGINAL PUBLISHING INFO:

PHILADELPHIA, PA.:
LUTHERAN PUBLICATION SOCIETY
COPYRIGHT, 1905,
BY THE
LUTHERAN PUBLICATION SOCIETY.

FOREWORD

A STATEMENT of so essential a Christian doctrine as that of the Atonement, in the full range and compass of its significance, and defended from the negative views now seeking to invalidate it, is certainly a pressing need of the times. It is the earnest attempt, at least, of this volume, to meet this want in our theology and devotional literature.

"Jesus Christ, with his pierced hands, lifted the gates of empires from their hinges and changed the currents of history,"—*Jean Paul Richter.*

CONTENTS

INTRODUCTION

DR. REMENSNYDER has written this book to commend the doctrine of the substitutive atonement of our Lord and Savior Jesus Christ. He has kindly asked me to say a few words by way of Introduction. It would be impossible not to comply with such a request. The battle in which Dr. Remensnyder has drawn his sword is the battle of every Christian man, and no one bearing the name of Christian has a right to refuse to do his part in it. It is quite true that Dr. Remensnyder writes from his own point of view, with which my own does not perfectly coincide. He is a Lutheran of the Lutherans—I am of the Reformed; and these two historical types of Christian thinking do not see quite eye to eye in all matters that concern even this central doctrine of Christianity. Were it my duty to follow him in all the details of his exposition, I am afraid, therefore, I should have occasionally to enter a somewhat emphatic dissent. But fortunately it is possible to differ in some things and yet heartily to agree in the main thing, and happily this is true in the present case. Lutherans and Reformed are entirely at one in their conception of the nature of our Lord's saving work as a substitutive sin-bearer and an atoning sacrifice, and of the vital importance of this conception for both Christian thought and Christian life. It would be a great pleasure to me if I thought I could say anything that would in the least degree add to the effect of Dr. Remensnyder's faithful reassertion of what he justly speaks of as "the heart of the Gospel," "the keystone of the Christian system," "the corner-stone of redemption."

The fact is that the views men take of the atonement are largely determined by their fundamental feeling of need, by what they most long to be saved from. They are, therefore, apt to conceive of the atonement in very broken and partial ways, corresponding to the evils which have been most poignantly brought home to their thought. From the beginning, well-marked types of thinking on the subject have accordingly been traceable. Men have been oppressed by the ignorance, or by the misery, or by the sin in which they have felt themselves sunk, or by the vague sense of incompleteness and limitation which belongs to them as finite creatures. They have, therefore, looked to Christ to deliver them now from the one and now from the other of these evils; and thus have conceived His work as consisting fundamentally in revelation of divine knowledge, or in the inauguration of a reign of happiness, or in emancipation from the limitations of individual existence, or in deliverance from the curse of sin. In the early ages of the Church's development, the intellectualistic tendency allied itself with the class of phenomena which we call Gnosticism; and the longing for peace and happiness which was the natural result of the crying social evils of the time found its most remarkable expression in what we know as Chiliasm. The vague aspiration toward absorption in something wider and higher than humanity we call Mysticism. That no such party-name suggests itself to describe the manifestation given to the longing to be relieved from the curse of sin does not mean that this longing was less prominent or less intense, but precisely the contrary. Each of the other views was recognized in its one-sidedness as a heresy, and received an appropriate designation as such. This view, on the contrary, was the fundamental point of sight of the Church itself, and, as such, was given expression in numberless ways—some of which appear somewhat strange to us, as, for example, the widespread representation of the atonement as centering in the surrender of Jesus as a ransom to Satan.

Our modern church is very much like the early church in all this. All of these tendencies are as fully represented in present-day thought as in any age of the Church's life. Perhaps at no other period, indeed, was Christ ever so frequently or so passionately set forth as merely the regenerator of society Certainly at no other period has His work been so prevalently summed up in mere revelation. The wonderful genius of Schleiermacher has given mysticism a vogue in the modern church such as it has enjoyed in no other age. But now as ever the hope of Christians at large continues to be set upon the Savior specifically as the Redeemer from sin, and wherever vital Christianity exists it exists by virtue of a clear and firm hold upon the basal fact of Christianity, declared by our Lord Himself and His apostles in the crisp formula that "Jesus Christ came into the world to save sinners."

The forms in which these differing types of thinking are clothed in our modern days are largely the result, of course, of the history of thought through the intermediate centuries. The assimilation by the Church of the doctrines of revelation was a gradual process; and it was also an orderly process—the several doctrines emerging in the consciousness of Christians for formal discussion and scientific statement in a natural, or, we might say, logical sequence. In this process, the doctrine of the atonement did not come up for formulation until the eleventh century, when Anselm gave it its first really fruitful treatment, and laid down for all time the general lines on which the atonement must be conceived, if it is to be thought of, in accordance with Scripture, as a work of deliverance from the penalty of sin. The influence of Anselm's discussion has been determinative on all subsequent thought down to today. Even the opposition to it has taken form and color from antagonism to it. Its extreme antithesis—the general conception that the atoning work of Christ finds its essence in revelation and had its prime effect, therefore, in deliverance from error—was advocated in Anselm's own day by perhaps the acutest reasoner of all the schoolmen, Peter Abelard. Later an intermediate view was powerfully set forth by Hugo Grotius. Mystical ideas always exist among us, but have never threatened to become dominant except perhaps during the short period when the influence of Schleiermacher reigned supreme. Broadly speaking, the field has been held practically by the three theories which are commonly designated by the names of Anselm, Grotius, and Abelard; and age has differed from age only in the changing expression given these three theories and the relative dominance of one or another of them.

The Reformers, it goes without saying, were enthusiastic preachers of the great Scriptural doctrine of "satisfaction" as given form by Anselm—of course as corrected, developed, and enriched by their own truer insight and deeper thought. Their successors adjusted, expounded, and defended the details of this doctrine, until it stood forth in the seventeenth century dogmatics in practical completeness. It is only true to say that during this whole period this conception dominated the entire thinking of the Church. Numerous controversies, it is true, raged about it; but these controversies were with Socinians and Mystics, rather than between recognized Church teachers themselves. It was only with the rise of Rationalism that a widely spread defection became observable. Under the blight which followed in the train of this great depression of Christian thought and feeling, men could no longer believe in the substitutive expiation which is the heart of the Anselmic doctrine, and a blood-bought redemption went much out of fashion. The dainty "Supranaturalists," or Semi-rationalists—who represented the higher reaches of Christian thinking in that sad day of coldness and shallowness in religion—could climb only to the height of the Grotian half-view, and allowed only a "demonstrative" as distinguished from an "ontological" necessity for an atonement, and an "executive" as distinguished from a "judicial" effect for it. It required the great upheaval of the revivals of the late eighteenth and early nineteenth centuries to restore the balance of Christian thought and enable men once again to recover the central doctrine of Christianity in its purity. This they effectually did; and it is probable that about the middle of the nineteenth century the doctrine of penal satisfaction had such a hold on the Churches that only an academic interest attached to the lower theories.

About that time a great change began, however, to set in, and once more the doctrine of a truly substitutive atonement came to be in wide circles first doubted and then scouted. At first voices like those of Hofmann in Germany, of Maurice and McLeod Campbell in Britain, then more radical notes like those of Bushnell and Ritschl were heard, until it became evident that a new flood of Rationalism was fully upon us. The immediate effect, of course, was to call out a powerful defense of the Scriptural doctrine; and our best treatises on the atonement come accordingly from this period. But the defense only stemmed the tide and could not roll it back. The ultimate result has been that the revolt from the conceptions of satisfaction, propitiation, expiation, sacrifice, reinforced continually by tendencies adverse to evangelical doctrine peculiar to our times, has grown more and more widespread, and in some quarters more and more extreme, until it has issued in an immense confusion on this central doctrine of the Gospel. Voices are raised all about us proclaiming a "theory" of the atonement impossible; while many of those who essay a "theory" seem to be feeling their tortuous way very much in the dark. That, if I mistake not, if we are to judge by the popular literature of the day, is the real state of affairs in the modern church.

Probably the majority of those who hold the public ear have definitely broken with the doctrine of a substitutive atonement. A tone of speech has even grown up regarding it which is not only scornful but positively abusive. Of course it is still in terms of the substitutive atonement that the humble Christian everywhere expresses the ground of his hope of salvation; and it is in its terms that the earnest evangelist everywhere still presses the claims of Christ upon the awakened hearer. There is no "life" in any other doctrine. But this does not deter "men of light and leading" from applying the harshest epithets to it, or pouring the strongest invectives upon it. "The whole theory of substitutional punishment as a ground either of conditional or unconditional pardon, is unethical, contradictory, and subversive"—that is the way those who study mildness of speech speak of it. If hard words broke bones, the doctrine of the substitutional sacrifice of the Son of God for the sin of the world would long ago have been ground to powder. The timeliness of a defense of this doctrine like Dr. Remensnyder's is therefore certainly obvious.

Let me try to set down in few words the impression which the most recent literature on the subject makes on me of what the modern world offers instead of the Scriptural doctrine of a substitutive atonement. We have already intimated that it is confusion that reigns here; and in any event I cannot go into detail. But it may repay us to observe at least in outline the driftage of recent teaching.

To obtain a just view of the situation, I think we ought to note, first of all, the wide prevalence among the sounder thinkers of the time, of the Grotian or Rectoral theory of the atonement—the theory, that is, that conceives the work of Christ not as supplying the ground on which God forgives sin, but only as supplying the ground on which He may safely forgive sin on the sole ground of His compassion. This theory has come to be the orthodox Arminian view and is taught as such by the leading exponents of modern Arminian thought whether in Britain or America; and he who will read the powerful argumentation to that effect by the late Dr. John Miley, say for example, will be compelled to agree that it is, indeed, the highest form of atonement-doctrine conformable to the Arminian system. But not only is it thus practically universal among the Wesleyan Arminians. It has become also the mark of orthodox Nonconformity in Great Britain and of orthodox

Congregationalism in America. Nor has it failed to take a strong hold also of Scottish Presbyterianism; and on the Continent of Europe it is widespread among the saner teachers. One notes without surprise, for example, that it was taught by the late Dr. Frederic Godet, though one notes with satisfaction that it was considerably modified upward by Dr. Godet, and that his colleague, Dr. Gretillat, was careful to correct it. In a word, wherever men have been unwilling to drop all semblance of an "objective" atonement, as the word now goes, they have taken refuge in this half-way house which Grotius has builded for them. I do not myself look upon this as a particularly healthful sign of the times. I do not myself think that, at bottom, there is in principle much to choose between the Grotian and the so-called "subjective" theories. It seems to me to be only an illusion to suppose that it preserves an "objective" atonement at all. But meanwhile it is adopted by many because they deem it "objective," and it so far bears witness to a remnant desire to preserve an "objective" atonement.

We are getting more closely down to the real characteristic of modern theories of the atonement when we note that there is a strong tendency observable all around us to rest the forgiveness of sins solely on repentance as its ground. In its last analysis, the Grotian theory itself reduces to this. The demonstration of God's righteousness, which is held by it to be the heart of Christ's work and particularly of His death, is supposed to have no other effect on God than to render it safe for Him to forgive sin. And this it does not as affecting Him, but as affecting men—namely, by awaking in them such a poignant sense of the evil of sin as to cause them to hate it soundly and to turn decisively away from it. This is just repentance. We could desire no better illustration of this feature of the theory than is afforded by the statement of it by one of its most distinguished living advocates. The necessity of atonement, he tells us, lies in the "need of some such demonstration of God's righteousness as will make it possible and safe for Him to forgive the unrighteous." Whatever begets in the sinner true penitence and impels him toward the practice of righteousness will render it safe to forgive him. Hence this writer asserts that it is inconceivable that God should not forgive the penitent sinner, and that Christ's work is summed up in such an exhibition of God's righteousness and love as produces, on its apprehension, adequate repentance. "By being the source, then, of true and fruitful penitence, the death of Christ removes the radical subjective obstacle in the way of forgiveness." "The death of Christ, then, has made forgiveness possible, because it enables man to repent with an adequate penitence, and because it manifests righteousness and binds men to God." There is no hint here that man needs anything more to enable him to repent than the presentation of motives calculated powerfully to induce him to repent. That is to say, there is no sign here of an adequate appreciation of the subjective effects of sin on the human heart, deadening it to the appeal of motives to right action however powerful, and requiring therefore an internal action of the Spirit of God upon it before it can repent; or of the purchase of such a gift of the Spirit by the sacrifice of Christ. As little is there any indication here of the existence of any sense of justice in God, forbidding Him to account the guilty righteous without satisfaction of guilt. All God requires for forgiveness is repentance: all the sinner needs for repentance is a moving inducement. It is all very simple; but we are afraid it does not go to the root of matters as presented either in Scripture or in the throes of our awakened hearts.

The widespread tendency to represent repentance as the atoning fact might seem, then, to be explicable from the extensive acceptance which has been given to the Rectoral theory of the atonement. Nevertheless much of it has had a very different origin and may be traced back among English-speaking teachers, at least, rather to some such doctrine as that, say, of Dr. McLeod Campbell. Dr. Campbell did not himself find the atoning fact in man's own repentance, but rather in our Lord's sympathetic repentance for man. He replaced the evangelical doctrine of substitution by a theory of sympathetic identification, and the evangelical doctrine of expiatory penalty-paying by a theory of sympathetic repentance. Christ so fully enters sympathetically into our case, was his idea, that he is able to offer to God an adequate repentance for our sins; and the Father says, It is enough! Man here is still held to need a Savior, and Christ is presented as that Savior, and is looked upon as performing for man what man cannot do for himself. But the gravitation of this theory is distinctly downward, and it has ever tended to find its lower level. There are, therefore, numerous transition theories prevalent—some of them very complicated, some of them very subtle—which connect it by a series of insensible stages with the proclamation of human repentance as the sole atonement required. As typical of these we may take the elaborate theory (which, like man himself, may be said to be fearfully and wonderfully made) set forth a few years ago by the Andover divines. This finds the atoning fact in a combination of Christ's sympathetic repentance for man and man's own repentance under the impression made upon him by Christ's work on his behalf—not in the one without the other, but in the two in unison. A similar combination of the revolutionary repentance of man induced by Christ and the sympathetic repentance of Christ for man meets us also in recent German theorizing, as, for example, in the teaching of Häring. It is sometimes clothed in "sacrificial" language and made to bear an appearance even of "substitution." It is just the repentance of Christ, however, which is misleadingly called His "sacrifice," and our sympathetic repentance with Him that is called our participation in His "sacrifice;" and it is carefully explained that though there was "a substitution on Calvary," it was not the substitution of a sinless Christ for a sinful race, but the substitution of humanity *plus* Christ for humanity *minus* Christ. All of which seems but a confusing way of saying that the atoning fact consists in the revolutionary repentance of man induced by the spectacle of Christ's sympathetic repentance for man.

The essential emphasis in all these transition theories falls obviously on man's own repentance rather than on Christ's. Accordingly the latter falls away easily and leaves us with human repentance only as the sole atoning fact—the entire reparation which God asks or can ask for sin. Nor do men hesitate today to proclaim this openly and boldly. Scores of voices are raised about us declaring it not only with clearness but with passion. Even those who still feel bound to attribute the reconciling of God somehow to the work of Christ are often careful to explain that they mean this ultimately only, and only because they attribute in one way or another to the work of Christ the arousing of the repentance in man which is the immediate ground of forgiveness. Thus we are told that it is "Repentance and Faith" that "change for us the face of God." And then, it is added, doubtless as a concession to ingrained, though outgrown, habits of thought: "If then the death of Christ, viewed as the culminating point of His life of love, is the destined means of repentance for the whole world, we may say also that it is the means of securing the mercy and favor of God, of procuring the forgiveness of sins." Again, we are told that Christ enters sympathetically into our condition, and gives expression to an adequate sense of sin. We, perceiving the effect of this, His entrance into our sinful atmosphere, are smitten with horror of the judgment our sin has thus brought on Him. This horror begets in us an adequate repentance of sin. God accepts this repentance as enough; and forgives our sin. Thus forgiveness rests proximately only on our repentance as its ground: but our repentance is produced only by Christ's sufferings: and hence, we are told, Christ's sufferings may be called the ultimate ground of forgiveness.

It is sufficiently plain that the function served by the sufferings and death of Christ in this construction is somewhat remote. Accordingly they quite readily fall away altogether. It seems quite natural that they should do so with those whose doctrinal inheritance comes from Horace Bushnell, say, or from the Socinian theorizing of the school of Ritschl. We feel no surprise to learn, for example, that with Harnack the sufferings and death of Christ play no appreciable part. With him the whole atoning act seems to consist in the removal of a false conception of God from the minds of men. Men, because sinners, are prone to look upon God as a wrathful judge. He is, on the contrary, just Love. How can the sinner's misjudgment be corrected? By the impression made upon him by the life of Jesus, keyed to the conception of the Divine Fatherhood. With all this we are familiar enough. But we are hardly prepared for the extremities of language which some permit themselves in giving expression to it. "The whole difficulty," a recent writer of this class declares, "is not in inducing or enabling God to pardon, but in moving men to abhor sin and to want pardon." Even this difficulty, however, we are assured is removable: and what is needed for its removal is only proper instruction. "Christianity," cries our writer, "is a revelation, not a creation." Even this false antithesis does not, however, satisfy him. He rises beyond it to the acme of his passion. "Would there have been no Gospel," he rhetorically demands—as if none could venture to say him nay—"would there have been no Gospel had not Christ died?" Thus "the blood of Christ" on which the Scriptures hang the whole atoning fact is thought no longer to be needed: the Gospel of Paul, which consisted not in Christ *simpliciter* but specifically in "Christ as crucified," is scouted. We are able to get along now without these things.

To such a pass have we been brought by the prevailing Gospel of the indiscriminate love of God. For it is here that we place our finger on the root of the whole modern assault upon the doctrine of an expiatory atonement. In the attempt to give effect to the conception of indiscriminate and undiscriminating love as the basal fact of religion, the entire Biblical teaching as to atonement has been ruthlessly torn up. If God is love and nothing but love, what possible need can there be of an atonement? Certainly such a God cannot need propitiating. Is not He the All-Father? Is He not yearning for His children with an unconditioned and unconditioning eagerness which excludes all thought of "obstacles to forgiveness?" What does He want but—just His children? Our modern theorizers are never weary of ringing the changes on this single fundamental idea. God does not require to be moved to forgiveness; or to be enabled to pardon; or even to be enabled to pardon safely. He raises no question of whether He can pardon, or whether it would be safe for Him to pardon. Such is not the way of love. Love is bold enough to sweep all such chilling questions impatiently out of its path. The whole difficulty is to induce men to permit themselves to be pardoned. God is continually reaching longing arms out of heaven toward men: oh, if men would only let themselves be gathered into the Father's eager heart! It is absurd, we are told—nay, wicked—blasphemous with awful blasphemy—to speak of propitiating such a God as this, of reconciling Him, of making satisfaction to Him. Love needs no satisfying, reconciling, propitiating; nay, will have nothing to do with such things. Of its very nature it flows out unbought, unpropitiated, instinctively, and unconditionally to its object. And God is Love!

Well, certainly, God *is* Love. And we praise Him that we have better authority for telling our souls this glorious truth than the passionate assertion of these somewhat crass theorizers. God *is* Love! But it does not in the least follow that He is nothing but love. He is Holiness and Righteousness as well; or, as our modern German friends love to express it, He is not "Love" barely, but "Holy Love," or, as we might as well say, "Loving Holiness." It may well be—to us sinners, lost in our sin and misery but for it, it must be—the crowning revelation of Christianity that God is love. But it is not from the Christian revelation that we have learned to think of God as nothing but love. That God is the Father of all men in a true and important sense, we should not doubt. But this term, "All-Father"—it is not from the lips of Hebrew prophet or Christian apostle that we have caught it. And the indiscriminate benevolencism which has taken captive so much of the religious thinking of our time is a conception not native to Christianity, but of distinctly heathen quality. As one reads the pages of popular religious literature, teeming as it is with ill-considered assertions of the general Fatherhood of God, he has an odd feeling of transportation back into the atmosphere of, say, the decadent heathenism of the fourth and fifth centuries, when the gods were dying, and there was left to those who would fain cling to the old ways little beyond a somewhat saddened sense of the *benignitas numinis*. The *benignitas numinis!* How studded the pages of those genial old heathen are with the expression; how suffused their repressed life is with the conviction that the kind Diety that dwells above will surely not be hard on men toiling here below! How shocked they are at the stern righteousness of the Christian's God, who loomed before their startled eyes as He looms before those of the modern poet in no other light than as "the hard God that dwelt in Jerusalem!" Surely the Great Divinity is too broadly good to mark the peccadillos of poor puny man; surely they are the objects of His compassionate amusement rather than of His fierce reprobation! Like Omar Khayyam's pot, they were convinced, before all things, of their Maker that "He's a good fellow and 'twill all be well."

The query cannot help rising to the surface of our minds whether our modern indiscriminate benevolencism goes much deeper than this. Does all this one-sided proclamation of the universal Fatherhood of God import much more than the heathen *benignitas numinis?* When we take those blessed words, "God is Love," upon our lips, are we sure we mean to express much more than that we do not wish to believe that God will hold man to any real account for his sin? Are we, in a word, in these modern days, so much soaring upward toward a more adequate apprehension of the transcendent truth that God is love, as passionately protesting against being ourselves branded and dealt with as wrath-deserving sinners? Assuredly it is impossible to put anything like their real content into these great words, "God is Love," save as they are thrown out against the background of those other conceptions of equal loftiness, "God is Light," "God is Righteousness," "God is Holiness," "God is a consuming fire." The love of God cannot be apprehended in its length and breadth and height and depth—all of which pass knowledge—save as it is apprehended as the love of a God who turns from the sight of sin with inexpressible abhorrence, and burns against it with unquenchable indignation. The infinitude of His love is illustrated not by His lavishing His favors on sinners without requiring an expiation of sin, but by His—through such holiness and through such righteousness as cannot but cry out with infinite abhorrence and indignation—still loving sinners so greatly that He Himself provides a satisfaction for their sin adequate to these tremendous demands. It is the distinguishing characteristic of Christianity, after all, not that it preaches a God of love, but that it preaches a God of conscience.

A somewhat flippant critic, contemplating the religion of Israel, has told us, as expressive of his admiration for what he found there, "that an honest God is the noblest work of man." There is a profound truth lurking in the remark. Only it appears that the work were too noble for man; and probably man has never compassed it. A benevolent God, yes: men have framed a benevolent God for themselves. But a thoroughly honest God, perhaps never. That has been left for the revelation of God Himself to give us. And this is the really distinguishing characteristic of the God of revelation: He is a thoroughly honest, a thoroughly conscientious God—a God who deals honestly with Himself and us, who deals conscientiously with Himself and us. And a thoroughly conscientious God, we may be sure, is not a God who can deal with sinners as if they were not sinners. In this fact lies, perhaps, the deepest ground of the necessity of an expiatory atonement.

And it is in this fact also that there lies the deepest ground of the increasing failure of the modern world to appreciate the necessity of an expiatory atonement. Conscientiousness commends itself only to awakened conscience; and in much of recent theologizing conscience does not seem especially active. Nothing, indeed, is more startling in the structure of recent theories of atonement than the apparently vanishing sense of sin that underlies them. Surely, it is only where the sense of the guilt of sin has grown grievously faint that men can suppose repentance to be all that is needed to purge it. Surely it is only where the sense of the power of sin has profoundly decayed that men can fancy that they can cast it off from them at will in a "revolutionary repentance." Surely it is only where the sense of the heinousness of sin has practically passed away that man can imagine that the holy and just God can deal with it lightly. If we have not much to be saved from, why, certainly, a very little atonement will suffice for our needs. It is, after all, only the sinner that requires a Savior. But if we are sinners, and in proportion as we know ourselves to be sinners, and appreciate what it means to be sinners, we will cry out for that Savior who only after He was perfected by suffering could become the Author of eternal salvation.

B. B. WARFIELD.

PRINCETON.

THE ATONEMENT AND MODERN THOUGHT

CHAPTER I

CHRISTIANITY AND THE MODERN SPIRIT

SECTION I. *Religion and Our Age*

OUR age is one of extraordinary mental activity. Never were there such large editions of popular books or such multitudes of readers. The natural tendency of this vast product of the press is to superficial thinking. The temptation is to be entertained at the expense of reflection. The stronger mental faculties are slighted, the deeper themes of thought unstudied.

Hence, our time is not a favorable one for religion. There is far less than there has been in the past of "seeing the invisible," of hearing the inaudible, and of musing upon the eternal. There is too little of looking by faith upon the realities of the spiritual sphere, of leading the still, deep, inner "life hid with Christ in God."

This demands a more serious age, men and women of finer moral sense and of sturdier mental brawn.

Nevertheless, it cannot be said that religion has lost its interest in our day. Amid all the worldly clamor and the commercialistic cries which fill the air, men find time for profounder thoughts. There is far more grave thinking and introspection of the soul in silent moments by the leaders in the secular marts than we often suspect.

And when we come to the philosophical, the literary, the theological, and the learned sphere, when has there been a deeper agitation and a keener discussion of religion? In fact, Christianity is the theme of the hour. Christ is the great storm-center. The Bible is the chief issue. The doctrines of Christianity are the battle-ground.

SECTION II. *Christianity on Trial*

We no longer live under the peaceful skies of our fathers, when there was a general acquiescence in Christianity. But the religion which has stood for centuries in Western civilization as the one only true heaven-given faith is under fire. On this and on that ground it is questioned. From manifold quarters comes the attack. Everywhere does Christianity find her position challenged. The faith of those who have been at ease is disturbed. Convictions not deeply rooted are shaken. Infidelity, President Harper tells us, is growing in the universities. Beyond question it is a crucial epoch for our holy religion, such as neither ancient, medieval, nor modern history has seen.

There are many causes for this, and as varied phases of the attack.

SECTION III. *Denial of the Supernatural*

Reason receives the natural alone. Faith perceives the invisible and believes the supernatural on divine testimony. Reason having failed to find God and immortality, it was left to revelation to make them known. For this the agency of the supernatural was necessary. Christianity accordingly stands or falls with the supernatural. God in giving the biblical revelation has miraculously interposed in the course of human history. Destroy the belief in its supernatural basis and element, and nothing distinctive of Christianity remains.

But ours is an era in which every attempt is made to discredit the supernatural. Science is here called upon to aid. The sphere of the scientists is the natural, and the marvelous advances made in the last century in the scientific realm have led many of its votaries to indulge an utterly false estimate of its claims. They have sought to make it monopolize the immaterial and supernatural, and to dictate terms to religion. But the scientist, with his spade and retort and telescope, can bring none of the spiritual world within his ken.

That is the sphere of man's higher faculties, of his spiritual sense. Science has achieved wonders to heighten the ease of living and to advance the power of man, but it cannot avail for that which is highest in man. It must remember that there is nothing in electric light to dispel the darkness of the mind, nothing in evolution to unveil God as a personal Spirit, nothing in the energy of radium to relieve the guilt of the soul.

This denial of the supernatural, whether in the name of reason or science, is the most destructive form of assault ever made upon Christianity. It is not a question of "specks in the marble of the Parthenon," but of the disintegration of its massive blocks and the downfall of the edifice. That a revelation has been given to men at all is denied. Jesus is but another Zoroaster; He is the foremost of a long line of illustrious moralists. The Bible is a grand volume indeed, giving utterance to the sublime thoughts of a noble group of ethical teachers. Henry Preserved Smith calls it a "book of moral edification." But it is not absolutely unique. Its supernatural inspiration is but a pious myth, a fraud of religious enthusiasts. It comes without objective authority from on high.

Hence, after the maxim of Coleridge, we are only to receive so much of it as divine as gets hold of us, *i.e.*, as is approved by our subjective reason. There is, therefore, no settled system of religious truth. The Church's doctrines are the mere teaching of men. The insistence upon faith in them is a demand of bigotry. To bow to this revelation as final is to narrow, to fetter the mind. Reason is the only supreme teacher. To escape from the authority of revelation is to drink the air of liberty, to soar into the sphere of freedom. Such is the issue joined. The crisis is the most elemental and dangerous in the history of Christianity.

"In the defense of supernatural Christianity everything is at stake. This is the reason that the crisis in which we are today is the greatest war of intellect that has ever been waged since the birth of the Nazarene."[1]

The battle, then, is one as to fundamental standpoints. The glossing over will not help us. Sweet assurances that we lose nothing by the modern theology must not satisfy us. "The faith of

---

[1] President Patton's Inaugural at Princeton Theological Seminary.

the men of Smith's type is not the evangelical faith of the Gospel. Satan has clothed himself today as the angel of scientific light and freedom, and is beclouding the spiritual vision of men. It is here where we must ask God to help us see clearly, and we dare not cry peace, peace, where there is no peace."[2]

Section IV. *Modern Thought Cannot Outgrow Essential Christian Truths*

That ours is an age of progress, of discovery, and of advance, often effecting a veritable revolution in human knowledge, is an argument weighing forcibly with many against Christianity. They say, "When we are finding so much false that we held true, and when we are leaving so many effete errors behind us, is it not natural that your Christian doctrines should be outgrown and superseded by others?"

Plausible as seems this argument, its fallacy is easily exposed. True progress is not made by destruction of the past, but by building upon it. If all that is old is false, then as soon as the new grows old it must be repudiated, and no truth remains—all progress is impossible. Conservatism is thus the only basis for progress, while radicalism, rejecting the rounds of the ladder of human ascent, ends in a destructive iconoclasm. It cuts from under its feet the only possible means of advance.

In the progress of the human race there are always fixed factors which cannot change. Amid the flux these abide settled. With these laws and invariable factors in all lands and times we have to deal. The ship builder in devising his vessel avails himself of the latest ideas, and how marvelous are the contrivances for speed, safety, and luxury of a modern steamer as compared with the clumsy hulks of half a century since. Yet certain primary conditions have not changed. He builds for the same seas, the same tides, the same laws of navigation as prevailed when Agamemnon sailed his simple craft of oar-manned vessels against the Trojans thousands of years ago. Amid all superficial variations, the course of nature, the orbits of worlds, the laws of angles, the principles of mathematics, the properties of atoms, the elements of art and

---

[2] Rev. J. A. W. Haas, D. D., in review of Prof. Henry Pre served Smith's Old Testament History.

beauty stand fast, as fixed by the divine ideal from the beginning of the creation.

Just so with moral and religious truths. The ethical principles authoritative over human action never change. So the essential needs of man for religion remain under all changes the same. His soul still hungers for God. Sin remains, and the need for redemption is as imperative as ever. Pain and sorrow and death have not been eliminated in the march of human progress, and so do men environed by these same foes require the same features and doctrines of Christianity to minister to their help and deliverance that their fathers did. Though theology may require a restatement of its truths to meet the changed conditions of the time, religion itself will not change. Of the fundamental, enlightening, regenerating, and redemptive doctrines of Christianity, the saying of Christ stands fast, "Heaven and earth may pass away, but my words shall not pass away."

Hamilton Wright Mabie fitly gives expression to this fact that progress can only be made by holding to the essentials as settled thus: "Whatever decay of former ideals and traditions his contemporaries may discover and lament, Browning holds to the general soundness and wholesomeness of progress, and finds each successive stage of growth not antagonistic, but supplementary to those which have preceded it."[3] To accord with the spirit of progress which characterizes our period, Christianity is not called upon to surrender or substantially change or mold anew her great distinctive doctrines, but contrariwise to hold fast to them.

And this very fact, that amid all the assaults made upon her tenets by a Celsus, a Porphyry, a Pelagius, an Arius, an Abelard, or by Greek Philosophy, or modern Rationalism, she has never compromised one jot or tittle her holy faith and testimony, accounts for her ability to retain her sway over so many varied ages of humanity, and so many diverse periods of culture, even down to the present hour. And this explains also why Christianity has ever been the source of mental, moral, scientific, and social progress, so that the nations that have owned her pre-eminence have walked in the light, while others have lain in darkness.

How the charge then disappears that conservative orthodox Christianity is a lock on the wheels of human advance, growth, and

---

[3] Essays on Literary Interpretation, p. 105.

progress. And how irrational likewise is seen to be the idea that Christianity must undergo a vital reconstruction to hold its place as the one only true religion!

SECTION V. *No Occasion for Alarm, but for Vigilance*

That a crisis confronts Christianity is not to be denied. Never has there been such a concert of energetic thinking directed against the cardinal tenets of the Christian faith. The peculiarity of the situation is that Rationalism within the Church is joining its hostile forces with those without. Secular thinkers treat orthodox Christianity with curt intolerance, assuming that the victory over it is already won. And with vast learning and immense painstaking, brilliant scholars, professedly Christians, are turning the fire of a destructive criticism upon the Bible. While declaring that their aim is to give us the "real message" of the Bible, and claiming a motive to honor it, they are insidiously destroying the main grounds upon which can rest any belief in its inspiration or any respect for its authority.

And constantly is it urged that we must look upon the Scriptures from a totally new standpoint, that Christian theology must undergo a radical reconstruction, and that the great and essential Christian doctrines must submit to cardinal modification. The Bible is simply a book of "moral edification." If Christianity will not thus adapt itself to the spirit of the age, we are told that it cannot survive, but will be relegated to the niche of an effete, outworn faith.

But let not the hearts of believers fail, nor let anyone waver in his firm, pure confession. It was meant that the kingdom of God should pass through just such crises as these. True faith is but purified and strengthened by the severity of the crucible. Time and again has the Church met such crises, when the powers of darkness have prematurely rejoiced, and when the hearts of Christians have grown faint. But ever has she issued forth victoriously from the peril and entered upon but a larger and more prosperous career. But the point for us to weigh is that this has not been effected without effort. Victory cannot be won by inertia, listlessness, and indifference. Attack must be met by defense. Sleepless aggressiveness must be resisted by untiring vigilance. Scholarship must be answered by scholarship. Specialists must be refuted by specialists. If we allow the citadel to be carelessly defended and exposed, we must not be surprised if it be taken by assault. It is a burning shame if the confessors of Christ will manifest less of interest, ardor and sacrifice, in standing up for His cause, than those exhibit who are bent on overturning it. At present, not only do Christians seem not to be sufficiently awake to the danger, but they are allowing to the enemy almost a monopoly of zeal and enthusiasm. One cannot but admire the patient, tireless study, and microscopical investigation which extremely latitudinarian critics are giving to every book of the Bible. The most difficult secrets of history are explored. The most improbable and impossible hypotheses are formulated. Every conceivable literary outfit is brought to play. Money is expended with the most lavish liberality. The press is used with unparalleled energy, and these negative views are circulated far and wide. They are touching and influencing every channel of current thought. Especially is the effort made to popularize them, to present them in such attractive guise as to win the ear and gain the mind of the public. The situation reminds one of a witticism of Henry Ward Beecher. In the hall of the Twin Mountain House in the White Mountains, where he spent his vacations, he observed a painting which represented a huge mastiff asleep, with a fine piece of meat between his paws, which an agile little cur was quietly and dexterously getting away with. "This scene," said Beecher, "fitly represents the conservatives and the radicals in religion. While the massive watch-dogs of orthodoxy are securely asleep, the vigilant poodles of destructive thought are stealing away the faith from the hearts of the people." Still there is no peril if we but do our duty, for God is on the side of Zion and its loyal servants. But the holy treasure of our faith can only be preserved by the fidelity, the learning, the mental effort and activity of its defenders. Christians must be awake to the emergency. They must think, must read, must have an intelligent acquaintance with the questions of issue, and must be quite as able to repel as others are to assail. They must call for and liberally support evangelical publications. It is but by thus "contending earnestly for the faith once delivered to the saints" that it can be maintained inviolate. And evincing this vigilance and "putting on the whole panoply of God," no one need have the least doubt or tremor as to the final issue. The Bible,

Christianity, and the Church will come forth from this crisis triumphant as from every other.

"The consideration of these questions we need not approach with the feeling of alarm that Holy Scriptures will be discredited or Christianity be overthrown by the revolutionary methods noticed in this volume. Christ still lives, and the Holy Spirit is no less active in the twentieth than He was in the first century. Wave after wave rises, lifts its crest on high, and breaks into thousands of fragments upon the rock on which the Church is built."[4]

[4] Dr. Henry E. Jacobs in Introduction to Haas's Biblical Criticism.

CHAPTER II

VITAL NATURE OF THE ATONEMENT

THAT the need of atonement is one of the most primary and deeply seated convictions of the human race is shown from its universality. It is witnessed to, not alone by revealed, but as well by natural religion. That man is fallen, that this has alienated him from the Deity, and that his sins must be atoned for before he can approach the throne of infinite justice is recognized even by the "religions growing wild." Thus writes Harnack: "That blood sacrifices are based on a deep religious idea is proved by the extent to which they existed among so many nations, and they are not, therefore, to be judged from the point of view of cold and blind rationalism, but from that of vivid emotion. It is obvious that they respond to a deep religious need."[5]

For this cause have altars everywhere reeked with blood, have living victims been offered up or caused to pass through supposed expiatory fires, have men voluntarily lacerated their bodies, and has the smoke of countless sacrifices ascended to the court on high. Eloquent testimony do these sacrificial rites and the prayers and rituals of all heathen religions bear to the supreme import this conviction has had for the race.

But what is thus vividly but often grotesquely shadowed forth in the heathen cults finds its complete and final expression in Christianity. No truth is more emphatically revealed in the Scriptures, none centers more directly in the person of Christ, and none is more integral to the Christian system.

What however differentiates Christianity from the nature religions is the unique feature that man, being impotent in his sin and fall to make atonement for himself, the propitiation proceeds

---

[5] What is Christianity? p. 157.

from the divine side and is made by the Son of God. It is as Shakespeare puts it:

> "He who best the vantage might have taken,
> Himself found out the remedy."

That this is the New Testament teaching, the Unitarian theologian, Martineau, admits: "One thing is certain to Paul: man, as he is, can answer no appeal for self-redemption, his present nature has long enough been tried and found wanting. The evils of his case arise from his constitution, and will never cease till he is reconstituted. Now that he has lost his Paradise, it is as vain to call for repentance as to cry, Turn ye, turn ye,' to the fallen angels flung from heaven! He can no more lift himself than the bird can fly without an atmosphere. Nothing short of a re-creation of him will be of any avail. The rescue, therefore, must come from superhuman power, the initiative must be with heaven, there must provision be made for the fresh departure."[6]

Hence to effect this redemptive work is the prime motive for which Deity becomes incarnate. "Christ Jesus came into the world to save sinners,"[7] affirms the great apostle to the Gentiles. It is that one far-off event to which the whole creation moves. As writes Fairbairn: "But the incarnation had a function, and so we must ask, *Cur Deus Homo?* (Why did God become man?) Whatever its function might have been in a sinless world, its purpose in ours was to save the soul from personal and the race from collective sin."[8]

Occupying this vital place in the body of Christian truth, it naturally is selected as a principal target of attack. So we find that against perhaps no other doctrine confessed by the whole Christian Church is there such a concert of hostile criticism as is now experienced by this one. It is either openly denied or so stated as to deprive it of any positive significance.

Now, as the atonement wrought out by our Lord and Savior Jesus Christ directly concerns each one's personal salvation, the interest attaching to it is not to be computed. The realization of the

---

[6] Seat of Authority in Religion, p. 476.
[7] 1 Tim. 1. 15.
[8] Place of Christ in Modern Theology, p. 479.

significance of the atonement is the most tremendous thing for every immortal soul.

And when so powerful and persistent an attempt is being made to tear from the Christian this great foundation of his faith, his peace and his hope, should he not give it his earnest thought, his anxious study and his strongest defense? With this end in view, the present volume is written, and for this purpose is the reader invited to the following inquiry into this vital Christian doctrine. Christianity is not an evolved, but a revealed religion. It is not the full-blown flower of the ethical faculty, but the appearance in the fullness of time of the divine scheme of redemption. It is super-historical, having been intervened by a supernatural series of events upon the course of history. These events constitute a revelation. The record of them is given in the Holy Scriptures. To these alone then can we go to ascertain the doctrines of the Christian religion. There is no other source or norm of Christian theology. Friend and foe alike admit these premises. And in the interpretation of Holy Scriptures we must be guided by sound and sane canons of critical exegesis. We cannot reject a text as uninspired or interpolated merely because it refuses to fit our preconceived theory. Nor can we rear a mountain of conclusion on a single text presenting an incidental phase of a doctrine, and then reject a hundred texts which give the primary and larger sense of the doctrine. Following these axiomatic principles, there is but one way for a Christian to ascertain the Christian doctrine of the atonement, and that is to go to the Scriptures.

CHAPTER III

SCRIPTURAL PRESENTATION OF THE ATONEMENT

No doctrine of Christianity is capable of more precise statement than the atonement. As the inspired writers regarded it as the central truth of the system, so it is shot in golden threads through the entire woof of revelation. It is presented in such varied forms and in such diversified phraseology as to develop it in broadest and minutest outline. It appears in the Old Testament under the figure of the ram which God provided as a substitute for Isaac in the scapegoat; and in the bloody and burnt offerings which Jehovah says "shall be accepted for the transgressor to make atonement for him."[9] The whole Levitical ritual is founded on the idea of sacrifice—shadowing forth in type the one great sacrifice to come.

The chief Old Testament word used for this purpose is כִּפֶּר (kipper) rendered by Gesenius "literally to cover over, with the purpose of hiding, blotting out—expiation, ransom, redemption."

The various words employed in the New Testament to set forth the doctrine are:

Sacrifice (θυσια), the thing sacrificed, the victim. "Jesus offered up once for all himself a sacrifice for sin" (Heb. 7:27). "But now once in the end of the world hath he appeared to put away sin by the sacrifice of himself" (Heb. 9:26), literally διὰ της θυσίας αὐτοῦ, *i.e.*, by means of His sacrifice. "For even Christ our passover (*i.e.*, our paschal lamb, with whose sacrificial killing the passover began) is sacrificed for us" (1 Cor. 5:7).

The idea in this term sacrifice is that of Jesus Christ the great High Priest of the human race submitting Himself to suffering and

---

[9] Lev. 1:4.

death as an atonement for sin, and as an acceptable substitute to God the Judge, that guilty man might escape.

Offering (τροσφορά), the general term of which θυσια is the specific. "Christ also hath loved us, and hath given himself for us an *offering* and a sacrifice to God for a sweet-smelling savor" (Eph. 5:2).

Ransom (Λύτρον). "Even as the Son of man came to give his life a ransom for many" (Matt. 20:28). "Who gave himself a ransom for all" (1 Tim. 2:6). On the meaning of λύτρον, Alford says: "Payment as equivalent for a life destroyed;" and Meyer remarks that "the use of ἀντι before it clearly marks the sense of λύτρον to be that of substitution and not of compensation only."

Propitiation (Ἰλασμος). "Jesus Christ the righteous is the propitiation for our sins" (1 John 2:2). "God loved us, and sent his Son to be a propitiation for our sins" (1 John 4:10). The idea involved in propitiation is a sacrifice offered to the divinity displeased and offended by sin, which averts His displeasure and disposes Him to graciousness toward the offender. How could that be called a propitiatory offering which did not propitiate, which did not ascend as a sweet-smelling savor, which produced no impression, effected no change in the attitude of the eternal Judge toward the sinner?

Redemption (Ἀπολυτρωσιν). That is, deliverance effected by purchase. Redemption from judgment entailed. Satisfaction made for our sin. "In whom we have redemption through his blood, even the forgiveness of sins" (Col. 1:14).

Reconciliation (ἰλάσκεσθαι), to expiate the sin, and thereby make God propitious to the sinner. Christ was "the high priest to make reconciliation for the sins of the people" (Heb. 2:17). That is, the high priest, by sprinkling the mercy-seat with the blood of the sacrifices, made expiation for the guilt of the people. But the great high priest, Jesus Christ, did this more effectually by the sprinkling of man's conscience with His own blood.

Atonement. This word is found but once in the New Testament (Rom. 5:11). "Our Lord Jesus Christ, by whom we have received the atonement." But it is not a literal rendering of the Greek word here used, viz. (καταλλαγῆν), which answers to the Hebrew כָּפֵר (kipper), occurring very frequently in the Old Testament in the sense of expiation. Thus it is used (Lev. 5:16): "If the soul commit a trespass, the priest shall make an atonement for him." Atonement, or at-one-ment, means to bring two who were alienated together, to make them one again. This rather expresses the effect of Christ's work than defines its nature. Satisfaction would be a more comprehensive word to characterize Christ's whole redemptive work. But atonement has come to be the generic term in use, and what it lacks in direct significance has been supplied by custom, so that it is not only popular, but fitly expressive.

Such are salient words portraying the Scriptural doctrine. These terms occur and re-occur in a host of passages, ever accentuating and giving fuller emphasis to their leading thought. Focusing them on one point, we have the great Scriptural truth of the atonement. It is that our Lord Jesus Christ suffered, shed His blood, died on the cross as an offering by means of which expiation was made for our sins, and a free and full atonement was purchased for us.

So reiteratively and cumulatively, then, is this doctrine taught and urged in the Scriptures that its sense is absolutely unmistakable. He that runs can read it.

The inspired writers were in no uncertainty as to that of which they wrote. The doctrine had been given them as an integral part of their message. It was as simple and clear in outline as it was vast and far-reaching in significance. It filled their minds with holy amazement. It thrilled their hearts with loving gratitude. It humbled and reproved their consciences. And with the strong energy of conviction, they—one and all—set it forth with such clearness, fullness, and harmony, as to leave no room for doubt or misconception of their meaning.

CHAPTER IV

CHRIST'S TEACHING AND THE ATONEMENT

THE Lord's death on the malefactor's cross was a fact that He knew well the apostles were not prepared to receive. Only gently did He disclose it to them as the dark shadows began to fall. And when He did forecast it, "Peter rebuked him, saying, Be it far from thee, Lord."[10] It was one of those paradoxes of His person and work which they "could not bear now," but were "to know hereafter." Then the Holy Ghost was to lead them, as He did lead Paul and Peter and John in their writings to look into far depths, hitherto hidden to them, of His redemptive death.

Nevertheless, Jesus taught His sacrificial death both indirectly and directly. *Indirectly,* in that He declared Himself to be the Messiah of the Old Testament, and that He specifically applied to Himself those prophetic delineations of the Messiah which declared that He should be the Suffering One, and be killed. So far from repudiating the Hebrew Christ as depicted by their holy seers, He declared that He fulfilled their predictions of Messiah's sacrificial death. Said He: "All things must be fulfilled which were written in the law of Moses, and in the prophets, and in the psalms concerning me. Thus it behooved Christ to suffer, that remission of sins should be preached in His name."[11] And no doubt He specifically expounded to them Isaiah 53, that "Golden Passional of the Old Testament," as setting forth His propitiatory death, for such direct exposition must have induced John to say of it: "These things said Isaiah when he saw Christ's glory and spoke of him."[12]

---

[10] Matt. xvi. 22.
[11] Luke xxiv. 46.
[12] John xii. 41.

But Jesus taught His atoning death *directly*. Matthew and Mark both give the passage: "Even as the Son of man came to give his life a ransom (λύτρον) for many."[13] On the signification of "ransom," Dr. Driver says: "Ransom is a propitiatory gift, but restricted by usage to a gift offered to propitiate or satisfy the avenger of blood, and so the satisfaction offered by a life."[14] Says Prof. Denny: "A ransom means unambiguously that the forfeited lives of many are liberated by the surrender of Christ's life."[15] Here Christ declares unambiguously and emphatically that His death was substitutional. As there is no reason to believe that He did not mean what He said, His declaration is final.

But in the strongest objective manner that language and picture could exhibit it did He also set forth the same idea in the institution of the Holy Sacrament. Of the fourfold iteration and identity of the solemn sacramental formula: "This is my body given, my blood shed for the remission of sins," Dean Stanley says: "These famous words thus form the most incontestable and authentic speech of the Founder of our religion."[16] No subterfuge of interpolation, no loose theory of inspiration, and no extreme method of the higher criticism can invalidate their force.

But two thrilling confirmations yet remain. When His soul was troubled by the near approach of His passion, and He prayed, "Father, save me from this hour," He checked the prayer with the reply, "But for this cause came I unto this hour."[17] That is, the great redemptive deed effected by His death was the secret of His incarnation. And so sharp was His struggle to meet this impending baptism that "His sweat was, as it were, great drops of blood falling down to the ground."[18] But can we conceive that Jesus was so appalled at the mere thought of physical death? If so, many a tender maiden, dying with unshaken bravery during the primitive persecutions, would have been superior to Him, who was to teach mankind how to live and how to die, and of whom Rousseau says: "If Socrates died like a man, Jesus died like a god!" How many a mere man, before and after Him, has met death in its most

---

[13] Matt. xx. 28 ; Mark x. 45.
[14] Hasting's Bible Dictionary, vol. iv., 128.
[15] Death of Christ, p. 45.
[16] Christian Institutions, p. 95.
[17] John xii. 27.
[18] Luke xx.ii.42.

excruciating forms without such an exhibition of weakness! But it was not the fear of physical pain. The agony in Gethsemane was a moral one. It was the consciousness in the Son of man that He was delivered up for our offenses, that He was suffering the penalty due our sin. "It was not the mere bodily death that He conquered—that death had no sting. It was this spiritual death which He conquered, so that at last it should be swallowed up—mark the word—not in life, but in victory."

The other seal is the awful cry of agony, to the verge of despair, on the cross: "My God! My God! why hast thou forsaken me?" There are but two ways of explaining this most dreadful outcry of horror that ever broke from human lips. One is that the crucified One was a deceiver or self-deceived, and that now the veil is torn off, His delusion is exposed, and He finds His life and mission a failure. The other is, that in identifying Himself with our fallen human nature, and making Himself an offering that the guilty world might escape, the Father juridically holds Him—the sinless One—as if guilty, and hides His face from Him. And under the awful sense of this alienation from His Father there burst from Him this cry of infinite woe.

This is the New Testament and Christian explanation of it, as defined by Paul in Galatians: "Christ hath redeemed us from the curse of the law, being made a curse for us."[19]

Every word and act, then, of our Lord relating to His death depict it as that sacrificial offering to which John the Baptist, with His sanction, bore witness, saying: "Behold the Lamb of God, which taketh away the sin of the world."[20]

---

[19] Gal. iii. 13.
[20] Ruskin, Seven Lamps of Architecture — Sacrifice.

CHAPTER V

VICARIOUSNESS OF THE ATONEMENT

A PLAIN reader of the New Testament, whose simple object was to get at the natural, grammatical sense of the words, could reach no other conclusion than that the principle of vicariousness lay at the heart of the Gospel.

Thus we read: "Whom God hath set forth to be a propitiation *through* faith in his blood."[21]

"Christ also hath once suffered *for* sins, the just for the unjust."[22] "For I delivered unto you first of all that which I also received, how that Christ died *for* our sins."[23] "The Son of man gave his life a ransom *for* many."[24]

In the above passages the following prepositions are used; διά, signifying "because of, on account of;" ὑπέρ, "in behalf of, for the sake of;" αντι, "in the place of, instead of;" περὶ, "because of, for the sake of."

These particles are employed in order to express by all possible shades of language the idea of substitution. They and the context in which they appear show that by no jugglery of words can the point be evaded that Christ's passion was vicarious.

Exegesis is here the greatest difficulty of those who oppose. The Bible is so full of a substitutionary atonement that the reader comes upon it everywhere. The texts which teach it are not rare and isolated expressions; they assemble in multitudes; they rush in troops; they occupy every hill and valley. "Without the shedding of blood there is no remission of sin," is the constant Scriptural

---

[21] Romans iii. 25.
[22] 1 Peter iii. 18.
[23] I Cor. xv. 3.
[24] Matt. xx. 28.

teaching. In the Old Testament it was "the blood of goats and calves," but in the New Testament, Christ, the High Priest, "by His own blood entered in once into the holy place, having obtained eternal redemption for us."[25]

For this purpose the eternal Son of God became incarnate. It was that He should assume our human nature that He might identify Himself with the race. Thus He was able to stand as their representative, to take their sins upon Himself, and in their stead to present an infinitely acceptable offering, to make a full atonement.

"As the work of one so constituted and representative of God and man the atonement is in its nature substitutionary. By setting forth Christ Jesus as propitiatory, through faith in His blood, God has shown forth His righteousness in the remission of sins, and proved Himself just, while the justifier of him who is of the faith of Jesus."[26]

So also writes Kuyper: "In all this He acted as our substitute. His burdening Himself with our sins was a high-priestly act, performed vicariously. Christ did not redeem us by His sufferings alone, but His passion was made effectual to our redemption by His life and voluntary obedience. That is, His *passive* and *active* satisfaction."[27] And says Hodge: "It is as clear as the sun that Christ suffered and died as our substitute, in order that we need not suffer what we deserved and in order that we, instead of dying, should be partakers of the life secured by His vicarious death."[28]

This is the absolutely unique and transcendent feature in Christ's great sacrifice that it is expiatory. In the Zend-Avesta; in the teachings of Confucius; in the doctrines of Buddha; and in the liturgic hymns of the Rig Veda, "mortify the body; crucify the desires; thyself must expiate thine own sins," is the best and utterly impotent advice that can be given the sin-smitten, guilt-burdened soul. But that Christ takes our place and renders that satisfaction which was beyond our power, and that God, for the sake of this incalculable offering, holds our expiation fully made, is the great distinctive characteristic of the atonement.

---

[25] Hebrews ix. 12.
[26] Fairbairn's Place of Christ in Modern Christian Theology, p. 486.
[27] The Holy Spirit in the Passion of Christ, p. 85.
[28] Systematic Theology, vol. ii., p. 543.

The Passover was a typical sacrifice in the realm of the natural, and Christ is a true sacrifice in the realm of the supernatural. "It is the sacrifice of the Lord's Passover" (Ex. 12:27). "Christ our Passover is sacrificed *for us.*" "Christ hath given himself for us, an *offering and a sacrifice* to God" (Ephes. 5:2). "When He said: Sacrifice and offerings, and burnt offerings, and offerings for sin, thou wouldst not, neither hadst pleasure therein; which are offered by the law; then said He, 'Lo, I come to do thy will, O God!' He taketh away the first that He may establish the second. By the which will we are sanctified through the *offering of the body* of Jesus Christ once for all."[29]

The attempt to interpret these passages in a figurative manner is entirely without warrant, and, even if legitimate, could not invalidate their meaning. For types and symbols are signs of realities. And what could these symbols of sacrifice signify if they did not all point to one great, veritable, and all-sufficient sacrifice? If the Biblical terms are at all to be interpreted according to the laws and usages and common intent of language, then they unmistakably set forth the vicariousness of Christ's offering.

---

[29] Heb. X. 8-10.

CHAPTER VI

OBJECTIVE EFFICACY OF THE ATONEMENT

A MARKED feature of modern Christian thought is the effort made to depict the atonement as merely subjective, that is, as a portrayal of divine love and compassion in so powerful a manner as to convict the conscience of sin and thrill it so deeply with the sense of the divine goodness as to lead by a purely natural internal discipline to sin's removal. No objective atonement, however, is made, no real substitution, no taking the sinner's place and bearing his load, is effected.

But this view altogether underestimates the New Testament teaching and empties it of its chief content. It entirely displaces that representative, vicarious element which is its distinctive feature. This view, indeed, has had its advocates, sporadically appearing from time to time, but orthodox Christianity has always held them to be heretical. Wrote the great church historian, Neander: "From the time of Anselm two opposing views of redemption were developed; the one viewed its method as objectively necessary, and derived its efficiency from this necessity; the other assigned rather a subjective connection to the two, as if it had been merely the pleasure of God to connect the price of redemption with the sufferings of Christ, because these were best adapted to effect the moral transformation of man."[30]

The atonement offered by Christ was objective. It was a genuine substitution. It was a veritable ransom. It was not visionary, but real. It was not a picture, but a drama. It was not shadow, but substance.

It was a true bearing of that load which bore man down to a depth from which he could not of himself rise.

---

[30] Hagenbach's History of Doctrines, vol. ii., p. 46.

Not alone Christ's specific teaching, but His whole bearing and demeanor, whenever He touched upon the theme, are irreconcilable with any other theory. It was that "He who knew no sin was made sin for us."[31] It was that He felt Himself as a substitute for sin, exposed to its measureless penalty. It was that "the Lord had laid upon Him the iniquity of us all."[32]

And because of this objectivity—because it was a fact and not a seeming—has the substitutionary offering of Christ positive power. It relieves the burdened conscience. It extracts the sting of guilt. It effects the forgiveness of sins. It brings, as St. Paul says, "Peace through the blood of the cross."[33] The atonement, no doubt, has a subjective side, a potent, indirect influence as exhibiting the love of God. This no such spectacle could fail to exert. But this is merely incidental and secondary. The objective is the primary and constitutive element.

The efforts of advocates of so-called modern thought and of the new theology, to hold to the orthodox terminology respecting the atonement, while emptying these terms of their intended significance by denying all substitutionary character, are an inexcusable juggling with language. Of this character are such statements as this of Professor Bowne:

"There is, then, no literal substitution of one person for another, no literal satisfaction of the claims of justice, no literal payment of a debt, no literal ransom or redemption, but a work of grace on our behalf which may be more or less well described in these terms. One who has been saved from sin and restored to righteousness and the divine favor may well think of himself as redeemed and ransomed, or as freed from debts he could never pay. And he might also well and truly think of his Savior as having offered Himself up as a sacrifice for him, as having died for him and redeemed him by His blood. But this is the language of emotion and devotion and gratitude and discipleship. It is the language of the Christian heart and life, not the language of theological theory."[34]

---

[31] 2 Cor. v. 21.
[32] Isa. liii. 6.
[33] Col. 1.20.
[34] The Atonement, p. 31.

A doctrine cannot be emotionally true while it is logically and actually false. The laity may be deceived by glittering generalities that are used to cloak specific denials of Christian truths. But champions of the faith should unsparingly expose such equivocal statements as being quite as disrespectful to the ordinary Christian mind as they are disloyal to the Scriptures.

CHAPTER VII

WAS IT CHRIST'S LIFE OR DEATH THAT ATONED?

IT is a modern tendency to place the emphasis on the life of Christ, and to minimize His death. This is a reversal of the New Testament presentation. There the forgiveness of sins is never connected with Christ's hunger, weariness, poverty, teaching, or any experience of His life, but is always placed in juxtaposition with His death. It is even as Paul writes: "For I delivered unto you, *first of all*, that which I also received, how that Christ died for our sins, according to the Scriptures,"[35] or, "Who was delivered for our offenses;"[36] or again, "That by means of death for the redemption of transgressions."[37]

Forrest, writing on "The Objective Element in the Redemptive Work of Christ," remarks: "The unanimous testimony of the apostles is, that the sacrifice of Christ as the ground of our forgiveness centers itself in His *death*. It is needless to quote passages. This idea is fundamental and pervasive."[38] And says Dale on the Atonement: "The importance of this conception for the writers of the Epistles is not to be measured by the number of times in which it is directly stated, but by the fact that it forms the presupposition on which they argue and appeal, and that its displacement would destroy the unity and coherence of their teaching."[39]

But chiefly significant is the fact that Christ Himself ever laid the main stress upon His death, His passion, and His blood, as the

---

[35] 1 Cor. xv. 3.
[36] Rom. iv. 25.
[37] Heb. ix. 15.
[38] P. 228.
[39] On the Atonement, chapters iv. and v.

all-important thing in His mission as the atoning Savior. He was ever pointing the reluctant disciples to it, and saying of it: "For this cause came I unto this hour."[40]

That Christ assumed our humanity and illustrated a *life* without sin does not lessen or remove man's sin, but rather accentuates its inexcusableness and guilt, and the more justifies God in its condemnation. Before, then, Christ could win the right to offer men release from sin, He must as their representative take away sin by the sacrifice of Himself. Hence "the apostles specifically ascribe the atonement to Christ's death. This was the culminating point of the offering, the final test of its completeness, the signal of the victory over Satan's power, the price paid for salvation, the moment which appeases the guilty conscience."[41] Christ could not save the world by thoughts, by truths, by teachings, by example. Mental enlightenment cannot remove judgment, cannot take away the sense of guilt, cannot bring freedom and peace. It only gives keener force to the edge of conscience. Christ must atone for sin by His sinless offering.

It is true, however, that the *death* of Christ would have been meaningless without His *life*. Without His foregoing incarnation, His exemplification of sinlessness, and His illustration of sonship with God, as our representative, His death in our stead would have been void of efficacy. "It came therefore upon Him," as Ritschl truly puts it, "in the fulfillment of His vocation," as the goal of His life. But to accentuate the life rather than the death is a misinterpretation of the Scriptural record, and an evasion of the reality of a propitiatory offering. The emphasis cannot be shifted from the cross to the incarnation. As Dr. Cremer, of the University of Greifswald, writes: "It is not the life which Jesus lived, but the death which He suffered, and toward which His whole life pressed that saves us."[42] And Martineau admits of the Epistle of the greatest of the apostles, "With the Pauline theology, the biography (*i.e.*, life) of Jesus is wholly subordinate, and the real divine economy opens with Calvary and concentrates all its light upon the cross."[43]

---

[40] John xii. 27.
[41] The Lutheran Cyclopedia, p. 29.
[42] Essence of Christianity, p. 29.
[43] Seat of Authority in Religion, p. 455.

CHAPTER VIII

THE ATONING BLOOD

THE idea of sacrifice was a chief constituent in the religion revealed by Jehovah to the Jews in the Old Testament. And this idea finds its cardinal expression in the use of blood. The blood of the slain animal was to be sprinkled upon the impure person, or to be put upon the horns of the altar, or, in the case of utmost solemnity, to be brought into the Holy of Holies and sprinkled upon the Mercy-seat. What was the significance of blood as thus the essential feature of the sacrifice? This is explained in the words of the Lord, thus: "For the life of the flesh is in the blood; and I have given it to you upon the altar to make an atonement for your souls; for it is the blood that maketh an atonement for the soul."[44] The principle is that man's life had been forfeited by his sin, and that it could only be saved by the substitution of another life. And as the life is bound up with the blood, with whose shedding the life goes out, so blood must be offered—life for life. "It was the blood, as the vehicle of the soul, which possessed expiatory virtue; because the animal soul was offered to God upon the altar as a substitute for the human soul."[45]

The offering had to be without fault or blemish, symbolizing the truth that the perfectly pure could alone atone for the impure. "It was provided that the life of a clean, spotless animal should be vicariously surrendered to God, and its blood, still quick and instinct with its soul, offered upon the altar. The atoning element resided in the blood."[46]

---

[44] Lev. xvii. n.
[45] Keil and Delitsch on Leviticus, p. 410.
[46] Lutheran Cyclopedia, p. 27.

The word commonly used in the Old Testament to describe the manner in which the blood effects this atonement means to *cover*, to hide, to put out of sight. Therefore, the blood is sprinkled upon the person, or altar, that the guilt may be covered over, shut out of God's holy sight, and His great displeasure thereby allayed. "The blood of sacrifice has thus quite a specific meaning. In it *the self-sacrifice of the offerer* is vicariously accomplished. Because man's incapability to enter directly into communion with God appears fresh at every offering, therefore every complete offering must be preceded by the *covering* of the atonement of blood, and, therefore, this is the condition, *sine qua non*"[47]

From this Old Testament usage we are prepared for the emphasis placed upon the blood of Christ in the New Covenant of grace, and its meaning and significance at once appear. The paschal lamb of the Jewish passover is but a feeble type of the sacrificial Lamb of God. "Neither by the blood of goats and calves, but by his own blood he entered in once into the holy place, having obtained eternal redemption for us."[48] He gives His holy and spotless life to redeem our sinful and guilty ones. He pours out His precious life-blood that with it He may cover and hide our sins from the All-Holy Eye. He makes peace between the offended God and condemned man, "through the blood of His cross."[49] This blood of the divine-human offering has power to relieve from the whole burden and penalty of guilt. "The blood of Jesus Christ, his Son, cleanseth us from all sin."[50] It not only reconciles God to us, but exerts a continuously and progressively cleansing effect upon us, as it chastens us with contrition for the suffering we have caused the innocent one. It is by means of this costly blood that we are "bought with a price,"[51] and that our great High Priest has made Himself "the propitiation for the sins of the whole world."

All through the New Testament runs this teaching of the atoning blood of the one great sacrifice. And the closing book represents a great throng approaching the throne of God in eternity, of whom it is said that they have "washed their robes and

---

[47] Oehler's Old Testament Theology, p. 280.
[48] Heb. ix. 12.
[49] Col. i. 20.
[50] I John i. 7.
[51] I Cor. vi. 20.

made them white in the blood of the Lamb."[52] "Here what is referred to is evidently the power of Christ's death to sanctify men—it was the power of His passion, descending into their hearts, which had made them pure, even as He was pure."[53]

The bloody sacrifices of Paganism are no true analogue of those of the Old, and of our Lord's sacrificial blood. For they are based upon a conception of the caprice, and rapacity, and cruelty of their gods, who must be appeased to allay their destructive dispositions. Still, in the main, they confirm the truth of the Christian idea of substitution. The serious-minded among the heathen feel that their guilt has alienated them from God; that thereby their lives are forfeited, and that nothing can remove this alienation, and restore them to divine favor, save another life. The Pagan sacrifices, then, are an adumbration of the sacrifice on Calvary. They are a sub-conscious seeking for the atoning blood of the Lamb. They are the testimony of natural to revealed religion. They are that witness of the Holy Spirit which St. Paul tells us gives some dim glimmerings even to the natural conscience of that "true Light which lighteth every man that cometh into the world."

It is, then, the immeasurably precious blood of the divine-human Savior in which lies atoning, redemptive power. "Through the blood of the cross He made peace; on the cross He blotted out the hand-writing which testified and testifies against us. In Jesus Christ we have forgiveness of sins through His blood."[54] For this divine balm of peace to the broken spirit and wounded conscience no modern ethical substitute can ever be found.

As writes President Patton, "If the Christian church is going to tie her fortunes to moral philosophy, God help her. We must go back to the religion of our fathers, to the atoning blood, or go on to pessimism, atheism, and despair." Let us then cling to the apostolic teaching: "Who gave himself for us (ὑπὲρ ἡμῶν) that he might redeem us from all iniquity, and purify (καθαρίζω, *i.e.*, cleanse by an expiatory blood offering) us unto himself."[55] It is this precious blood which has a practical power to move and renew the

---

[52] Rev. vii. 14.
[53] Denny, Death of Christ, p. 247.
[54] Cremer, Reply to Harnack on the Essence of Christianity, p. 21.
[55] Titus ii. 14.

hearts of men, as has no truth out of Scripture, and none other in it.

A missionary in China says: "If there is anything that lays hold of the people here, it is the simple story of the crucifixion of the Lord Jesus Christ. Not His miracles, nor even His wonderful sayings or teaching, but the old, old story of the cross, *of the blood*, of the sacrifice, of the satisfaction of Christ in dying for sinners on the tree—that is the power for good in touching the heart and awakening the conscience."

And this is confirmed by the experience of all Christian workers, whether abroad or at home.

CHAPTER IX

DID CHRIST SUFFER THE PUNISHMENT OF SIN?

THE question is often raised in current inquiry whether Christ bore the punishment of sin, or, in other words, "Did God punish Jesus Christ?"

The Scriptures teach that Christ bore our sins. "The Lord hath laid on him the iniquity of us all."[56] "Who his own self bare our sins in his own body on the tree."[57] Now there are only two ways in which this could be done. Namely, by bearing the guilt or the punishment. But one involves the other. Guilt entails punishment. Transgression carries with it, as an inseparable factor, penalty. Guilt and punishment grow out of one stem. If then we say that Christ bore our sins in the sense that He took upon Himself their guilt, it is none the less reasonable to affirm that He endured their punishment.

And the Scripture passages directly affirm this as a part of the atonement. We are told that Christ "*suffered* for us;" "He tasted death for every man,"[58] *i.e.*, the sharpness of death as the penalty of sin. That He was "wounded for our transgressions," that "the chastisement of our peace was upon him," and "by whose stripes," says St. Peter, "we were healed."[59] When then Lyman Abbott says that "we can adduce no passages which speak of Christ undergoing the punishment of sin," the assertion is in the teeth of the facts. And if he is willing to admit that Christ bore the guilt of sin, this is the more difficult horn of the dilemma, since to suffer one's punishment is far more conceivable than, being innocent, to feel

---

[56] Isa. liii. 6.
[57] 1 Peter ii. 24.
[58] Heb. ii. 9.
[59] 1 Peter ii. 24.

his guilt. Yet Christ did feel the guilt of sin. This was the very sword that pierced His soul, and wrung from Him the awful cry on the cross, which Canon Gore says was the "trial of the righteous man forsaken."[60]

Christ was not indeed guilty, yet the atonement could have had no value had He not voluntarily assumed our guilt. And thus taking our place, God had to hold Him as if guilty, to hide His face from Him, and "He had to suffer as our representative the penalty of God's displeasure at human sin, and to acknowledge it to be just."[61] God in His justice had to punish the sinner. The penalty for the violation of the law is death. The sinner or his substitute must die. Christ, sinless and guiltless, yet offered to bear the guilt and punishment of sin, and thereby became the great atoning sacrifice. "We are bought with a price."[62] "Purchased with his own blood."[63]

"It seems to have been assumed by the Christian fathers of Anselm's time that punishment or suffering in some form constituted the inmost quality of the offering which satisfied the justice of God."[64] So Luther, speaking of the darkness and agonized outcry of forsakenness at the cross, says: "It is *punishment* which God here suffers to come upon His Son. The Lamb of God bears our sins, and bearing is rightly interpreted as being punished. He is punished just because He has assumed our sins, and God, on the other hand, must, therefore, assume toward Him the attitude of an enemy."[65]

And Dr. Hodge writes: "The satisfaction of Christ was penal. What the church teaches when it says that Christ satisfied divine justice for the sins of men is that what He suffered was a real adequate compensation for the penalty remitted; He satisfied justice. But He did not suffer either in kind or degree what sinners would have suffered. In value His sufferings infinitely transcended theirs. The death of an eminently good man would outweigh the annihilation of a universe of insects. So the sufferings and death of

---

[60] Bampton Lectures, pp. 148, 149.
[61] Forrest, The Christ of History and Experience, p. 238.
[62] I Cor. vi. 20
[63] Acts xx. 28.
[64] Allen's Life of Matthew Edwards.
[65] Commentary on Gal. ii. 16.

the Son of God immeasurably transcended in worth and power the penalty which a world of sinners would have endured."[66]

---

[66] Systematic Theology, vol. ii., p. 471.

CHAPTER X

IS GOD RECONCILED TO US?

ONE of the most common methods of stating the atonement in Scripture is by the term "reconciliation." It is looked at from the standpoint of an estrangement between God and man, which the propitiation of Christ removes and there results a blessed reconciliation. Thus it is said that "God was in Christ reconciling the world unto himself, not imputing their trespasses unto them."[67] Again: "For if when we were enemies we were reconciled to God by the death of his Son; much more, being reconciled, we shall be saved by his life."[68] So, by pre-eminence the office of preaching the Gospel is called "the ministry of reconciliation."[69]

Now, it is often contended by current critics that this reconciliation in no sense affects God, that it is wholly on man's part, and that God does not need to be reconciled; that His attitude to the sinner ever remains the same. But the Scriptures represent man as being, in his fallen state, under the curse of God. "Christ hath redeemed us from the curse of the law, being made a curse for us."[70] Again, we are declared to be under the wrath of God and in extreme danger from it. "Being now then justified by his blood, we shall be saved from wrath through Him."[71] We thus see that on one side the sinner is steeped in guilt, and on the other God is wronged, displeased, and threatens judgment. His law has been violated and His love injured. Christ thereupon making propitiation, the sinner's guilt is replaced by innocence, and the divine displeasure

---

[67] 2 Cor. v. 19.
[68] Romans iv. 10.
[69] 2 Cor. v. 18.
[70] Gal. iii. 13.
[71] Romans v. 9.

is displaced by graciousness. The reconciliation hence is mutual. It is not, indeed, that God has changed in His essential nature, but He has changed in this that His love is able actively to assert itself instead of His justice.

When a son falls into vice and his father refuses to see him, if the son then returns and a reconciliation results, we do not properly say that the son is reconciled to his father, but the son has changed morally, has repented, while it is the father who has been *reconciled* through the repentance. It may be true, as Bishop Westcott says, that "such phrases as 'propitiating God' and 'God being reconciled' are foreign to the language of the New Testament." Nevertheless, these New Testament expressions themselves are sufficiently indicative of their meaning. Propitiation is not offered to the transgressor, but to the judge. To contend that these passages mean that the sinner is to be propitiated, and not God, is the absurdity of exegesis. So also it is the injured and affronted Father who is to be reconciled, and not the offending prodigal who is graciously to regard his parent again. And the means of this reconciliation is the propitiatory sacrifice of Jesus Christ.

The emphasis, of course, is laid upon the part of man, on whose side are the wrong-doing and the needed propitiation. Hence when God is portrayed as hiding, then showing His face; as launching His curse, then exercising His mercy; as insisting on propitiation before there can be peace; we see that this reconciliation has a divine as well as a human side.

God has not, indeed, been reluctantly won to mercy. It is the mercy which is the source of the propitiation, not the propitiation which is the source of the mercy. But without this propitiation God would have regarded the sinner not as a son, but as an enemy, and there could have been no reconciliation. "We believe there is a sense in which God needed to be reconciled; not that His anger had to be appeased or placated, as if He were resentful or vindictive; no, no, but that His justice had been outraged, His righteous laws trampled upon, and therefore satisfaction had to be rendered before mercy could have a free channel in which to flow down to man the sinner."[72]

---

[72] Dr. L. S. Keyser.

To deny this divine side of the reconciliation on the plea of exalting the unchanging love of God is to ignore that attribute of righteousness which is essential to His moral nature and to His perfect personality. "We know," writes Kuyper, "that this is called the *juridical* conception, and that in these effeminate days men desire to escape from the tension of the right; therefore the ethical conception is lauded to the skies. But this opposition to the juridical conception sets God at naught and grieves Him. The ethical idea is: 'I am sick; how can I become well?' The juridical idea is: 'How can God's violated rights be restored?' The latter is therefore of primary importance. I must first acknowledge the living God, and that He has righteous claims upon me, which I have violated and which must be satisfied."[73]

Where there is this deep conception of sin, not only as evil in the sinner, but as guilt, as wrong-doing to God, as doing Him an injury which turns Him away from and against the transgressor, there will be the conviction that God must first be reconciled by an atonement before the repentant sinner can be reconciled to Him.

"Because God's anger is a holy anger it requires that atonement shall be made for sin. God, according to His own nature, requires a satisfaction to be made for sin. In the idea of atonement for sin the willingness of God to pardon the sinner must be presupposed as already existing. God's character requires, not that this willingness shall be awakened by the atonement, but that the moral possibility shall be presented for putting it into effect."[74]

---

[73] The Work of the Holy Spirit, p. 270.
[74] Rothe's Still Hours, p. 230.

CHAPTER XI

THE CENTRAL PLACE OF THE ATONEMENT IN CHRISTIANITY

IT occupies the chief place. It is the burden of the New Testament. It is the heart of the Gospel. It is the keystone of the Christian system. It is the central truth of Christian theology. It is the corner-stone of redemption. Remove this foundation, and the whole edifice crumbles to ruin. There is no Scripture truth or doctrine of Christian theology which does not bear more or less a relation of dependency upon it. Everywhere the death of Christ is the most intense focus of His life, and every other feature of His life and work is made subsidiary to the fact that He came to make an offering unto death for sin. "Christianity, which God consents to offer to the world, is the forgiveness of sins in the blood of Christ."[75]

First, it is inseparably interwoven with the *incarnation*. When it is written: "For as much as ye know that ye were redeemed with the precious blood of Christ, who verily was foreordained before the foundation of the world,"[76] we learn that the purposes of incarnation and redemption were cotemporaneous in the divine thought. Evidently "Christ was made in the likeness of man, that he might become obedient unto death, even the death of the cross."[77] In all probability the Son of God would never have become incarnate had it not been for the purpose of the atonement. And it would appear that the very creation of man was conditional upon this divine idea. God would not have created man had it not been that, foreseeing His fall, a Savior was foreordained, to counteract the tragic event. The great wonder of the incarnation with all its

---

[75] Cremer, The Essence of Christianity, p. 266.
[76] I Peter i. 20.
[77] Phil. Ii. 7, 8.

attendant glories, and the very creation itself, are bound up in the atonement. All belong together as integral parts of a higher cycle of events than those within the ordinary range of human experience. Whoever has believed and experienced that inconceivable miracle—the fact of our redemption—has experienced Jesus, and lives in the realization that He is ours, and belongs to us as no one else can belong to us; to Him the miracle of His resurrection, and consequently the wonder also of His incarnation, is not too great.

The atonement, further, is the correlative of the Scriptural doctrine of *sin*. Sin, in its light, is seen as that desperate reality in God's world, requiring a supreme and mysterious sacrifice for its removal. What would Christian theology do with the hideous factor of sin were it not for the justifying blood of Christ? But wherever in the pages of the New Testament "sin reigns unto death," there side by side "grace reigns unto eternal life by Jesus Christ our Lord."[78]

God's noblest moral attribute, *love*, depends upon the atonement for its crowning illustration. Without the atonement, the brightest luster of infinite goodness and compassion could not have been revealed to the wonder and adoration of men and angels.

The *divinity* of our Lord is conditioned by it. For, to render a satisfaction which humanity was impotent to do, there must be an offering sinless and of infinitely precious worth. This involved the sacrifice of one who was divine, and whose sacrifice would, therefore, have an all-prevailing potency.

Again, it necessitates the doctrine of the *Trinity*. Without this mysterious feature in the secret being of the Godhead, the atonement would be inconceivable. As it was God who must be propitiated, and God who alone could make the propitiation, there arises the necessity for the persons of Father and Son in the undivided divinity, which finds its trinal perfection in the procession of the third personality, the Holy Spirit, without whose life-giving agency there could be no application of the purchased redemption to man "dead in trespasses and in sin."

It bears directly upon that great doctrine upon which Luther built the Reformation, and which he called the doctrine of a standing or falling Church—*Justification by Faith*. For since Christ

---

[78] Rom. v. 21.

by the sacrifice of Himself has paid the full penalty of sin, there needs but for the sinner by faith to make this satisfaction his own, and his debt is paid, and he stands forth justified before God.

It gives us, too, the only satisfactory solution of the *death of Christ*, of the mystery of the cross, of the suffering of the Son of God, which else would be an insoluble enigma. The redemption of men turns that awful hill of despair and deicide into the highest glory-crowned mount of time.

It points also to the *resurrection* which must needs follow, to vindicate with power the atoning sufferer as divine.

And it is essential to the *Lord's Supper*, which owes to it its elements, "the bread broken for you," and the "blood shed for the remission of sins."

And this necessitates the *Church* with its word and sacraments as means of grace, whereby the Holy Spirit works to the efficacious use of the great salvation.

The essential Christian doctrine then is that of an objective atonement. "The message of the apostles proclaimed to the world finds its central thought to be forgiveness of sins through a crucified, divine Savior. Paul declares that he will know nothing save Jesus the crucified, through whose blood we have the forgiveness of sins. John rejoices that the blood of Christ cleanseth from all sin. Peter says, 'Ye know that ye were redeemed with the precious blood of Christ.' This is their constant insistence."[79] So writes Dr. Denny in his recent book: "The propitiatory death of Christ, as an all-transcending demonstration of love, evokes in sinful souls a response which is *the whole of Christianity*. The process which starts with rejecting the objective atonement has its natural and inevitable issue in the denial that Christ has any essential part in the Gospel. We can only assent to such a view by renouncing the New Testament as a whole."[80] Speaking of the attempt of some to substitute for it, in deference to modern critical thought, what is called an "up-to-date Gospel," the venerable Dr. Cuyler says: "This age of ours, with all its mighty mechanical inventions and its increasing mammon-worship, has not advanced one single inch beyond its indispensable need of the atoning blood of Jesus and the converting power of the Holy Spirit. All the

[79] Cremer, Essence of Christianity, p. 47.
[80] The Death of Christ: Its Place and Interpretation in the New Testament.

telegraphs and the telephones, and all the universities, with their boasted achievements in scholarship, have not yet outlawed Calvary and Pentecost. Human nature has not changed; human sinfulness and sorrows have not changed; the Word of God has not changed; the precious promises have not changed; and what fallen man needed to lift him Godward nineteen hundred years ago he needs today. Stick to the old Gospel. When God gives you another, preach it, but not before."

The atonement, therefore, is the heart of Christian theology. The cross is the center of the universe. It is the point around which all the great events of human history revolve. Not alone the theologian, but the philosopher and the historian must take their points of view from Calvary. As well tear the bones from the body, or pluck the sun from the solar system, as to ignore or strike out the atonement from Christianity.

CHAPTER XII

UNIVERSALITY OF THE ATONEMENT

THE Scriptures represent God as a Father loving all His children. When Ephraim goes astray, He calls after him with tender compassion. The Parable of the Prodigal Son shows that even in sin and shame, the Father's heart still holds a place for the erring one. So, when the eternal Father wills to send His Son on a mission of redemption, its purport is thus defined: "God so loved the *world* that he gave his only begotten Son."[81] Again: "And he is the propitiation for our sins; and not for ours only, but also for the sins of the whole world."[82] "I, if I be lifted up from the earth, will draw all men unto me."[83] So Paul argues that the righteousness of Christ, "the free gift, came upon all men unto justification of life."[84] And Peter tells us that "the Lord is not willing that any should perish, but that all should come to repentance."[85] In Heb. 2:9 we have the strong expression, "Christ tasted death for every man."

These passages are so specific that we cannot mistake their meaning. They show that the divine scheme of redemption was comprehensive and universal. Christianity was no longer to be a national religion, like that of the Jews, but was to embrace all nations and races. Wide as sin reigned and wide as the curse prevailed, salvation was to abound. It is toward man, in his low estate, that the heart of the Infinite moves with saving love. The atonement is universal.

---

[81] John iii. 16.
[82] 1 John ii. 2.
[83] John xii. 33.
[84] Rom. v. 18.
[85] 2 Pet. iii. 9.

There is indeed another class of passages which teach the doctrine of an election such as Ephes. 1:4, 5: "Even as God chose us in Christ before the foundation of the world—having foreordained us unto adoption of sons through Jesus Christ unto himself, according to the good pleasure of his will." While these passages must be recognized and weighed in their full significance, they must not be so construed as to weaken or invalidate the ones previously quoted. But both must be explained by the principle of the analogy of faith, so as to find the basal truth in which they harmonize.

Accordingly neither Calvinists, who base this election on the sovereign decree of God, nor Lutherans, who base it on the prevision of faith, deny the universality of the atoning death of Christ. Thus wrote Dr. Hodge: "Augustinians do not deny that Christ died for all men. What they deny is that He died equally and with the same design for all men...He was a propitiation effectually for the sins of His people, and sufficiently for the sins of the whole world."[86]

And writes the Lutheran, Dr. Jacobs: "The Scriptural doctrine of Predestination, while claiming for God the sole glory and making Him the sole cause of man's salvation, is most carefully guarded from all Fatalism, since every elect and regenerate man could by his own will be otherwise than he is, while it is alone by God's will that he is as he is."[87]

Prof. Edwards A. Park, seeking to find a common ground between the parties, wrote: "One party contemplate men as passive receivers of sanctifying impressions; and their question is, 'How many did God intend by regenerating influence to make partakers of the benefits of the atonement?' The answer is, 'The elect.' And so say we. The other party contemplate men as moral agents; and their question is, 'How many did God intend to furnish with a means of pardon which they should be under obligation to improve for their everlasting good?' The answer is, 'All who hear the Gospel.' And so say our brethren."[88]

We touch indeed here one of the profoundest of mysteries—the reconciliation of human freedom with Divine Sovereignty. This

---

[86] Systematic Theology, vol. ii., p. 558.
[87] Elements of Religion — God's Eternal Purpose, p. 78.
[88] Extent of the Atonement, p. 252.

same difficulty which encounters the acutest philosophical thinkers in their endeavors to solve the riddle of the spiritual universe is reflected in the Scriptural treatment of the theme, where man's free will and God's initiative and absolute control are alike emphasized. Seeking to solve it, we are like Milton's great debating spirits in Paradise Lost, who

> "Reason'd high
> Of Providence, Foreknowledge, Will, and Fate;
> Fixed Fate, Free Will, Foreknowledge absolute;
> And found no end in wandering mazes lost."

The mystery we can safely leave to the hour when we shall no longer "see as through a glass darkly."

For us it is but to hold to the clear and emphatic teaching of Scripture that the atonement is of universal application, and that each one is responsible if he fail to accept the offer of grace. That God has so loved the world in its fall and guilt and shame as to resolve to save it, that from eternity there issued the decree which was to circumvent sin and death, and that all are called upon to believe, repent, and be saved through the offering of our Lord Jesus Christ—this is the great blessed truth of the atonement.

In conclusion, the Scriptural teaching as to the universality of the atonement, as expressed in the declaratory statement attached to the Revised Westminster Confession of Faith, is one that we can all endorse: "That, concerning those who are saved in Christ, the doctrine of God's eternal decree is held in harmony with the doctrine of His love to all mankind, His gift of His Son to be the propitiation for the sins of the whole world, and His readiness to bestow His saving grace on all who seek it. That, concerning those who perish, the doctrine of God's eternal decree is held in harmony with the doctrine that God desires not the death of any sinner, but has provided a salvation sufficient for all, adapted to all, and freely offered in the Gospel to all; that men are held responsible for their treatment of God's gracious offer, and that no man is condemned except on the ground of his sins."

All then can join in Zinzendorf's hymn of praise for that redeeming love provided for all, offered to all, able to save all:

> Lord, I believe were sinners more
> Than sands upon the ocean shore,

Thou hast for all a ransom paid,
Thou hast a full atonement made.

CHAPTER XIII

NO UNIVERSALISM IN THE ATONEMENT

THE universality of the atonement, the efficacy of the satisfaction rendered by Christ, does not by any means prove a like universality in its practical effect. The free salvation it provides is not indeed limited, but that is a very different thing from saying that it is not conditioned. This it, indeed, is everywhere. The atonement demands a moral test. It is not a magical work, transforming the sinner without the consent of his will. Nor is it to be mechanically taken hold of as one would appropriate the possession of a fortune. But its reception is dependent upon a certain spiritual state. "Whosoever believeth" is its invariable condition. There must be a voluntary reception of the unspeakable gift.

And where this is refused, where men deliberately turn away from the Crucified, where God's surpassing grace is rejected, there the universal salvation does not become universally effective. "He that believeth on the Son hath everlasting life; and he that believeth not on the Son shall not see life."[89] The sin which we are "not to pray for;" the "sin for which there is neither forgiveness in this world nor in the world to come;" the "impassable gulf" fixed between the two future states; and our Lord's fateful declaration of an everlasting punishment; make wholly untenable, from any Scriptural standpoint, the doctrine of universalism as involved in, or deducible from, the universality of the atonement.

Universalism as a denomination is a total failure. Its numerical adherents are utterly insignificant as compared with the overwhelming strength of the orthodox churches. This meagre outcome is probably owing to the general conviction as to the

---

[89] John iii. 36.

injurious moral results of a teaching devoid of a positive moral authority. "The preaching of the Universalists," says Baird's Religion in America, "positively exercises no reforming influence on the wicked, and what worse can be said of it?" Yet it is a contention of the Universalists that their doctrines are insidiously growing in the orthodox churches among many, especially ministers, who decline publicly to avow them. While unsubstantiated claims of this character, as so often made, are, as a rule, unwarranted, yet it cannot be denied that the arguments of many, who, like Farrar, place all the emphasis on the love of God, while quite ignoring His justice,—as the backbone of the moral universe,—do tend strongly in that direction.

And the Scriptural doctrine of the atonement, so far from countenancing this line of liberal thought, is the most irrefutable disproof of it. For, if the atonement sets in a most surpassing luster the divine love, not a whit less vividly does it portray the inexorability of the divine attribute of justice. A God, who from His regard to the inflexible sovereignty of moral law, will spare not His only Son from the shame and agony of the cross, when He appears as a substitute for sinners, will not either spare the guilty, who reject "the only name under heaven given among men, whereby we must be saved."[90] In fact, the very last doctrine in the Scripture in which universalism can find any support is that of the atonement.

---

[90] Acts iv. 12.

CHAPTER XIV

THEORIES OF THE ATONEMENT

RELIGIOUS truths have a history analagous to physical facts. At first, as these are discovered, they exist in loose disorder, without connection or arrangement. But by degrees, as their qualities and relations are labeled, they are classified in their true order, and form a science. A satisfactory theory of them can then be formulated. Such has been the procedure with religious truths. At first the Christian tenets were held simply as isolated facts. But by degrees they came to be apprehended in a larger view, so that they could be arranged into a grand harmonious system, and an intelligent theory of them be formulated.

By this process has issued the science of Biblical theology. Such has been the evolution of all Christian doctrine. And so of the Atonement. The early Christians and church fathers held it positively, without any attempt to state it in formal terms. The first definite theory of it was that originated by Anselm. This was, that when man by his fall had broken the divine law, violated the honor of God, and become alienated from Him, it was necessary that Christ, as God-man, by voluntary submission to the penalty of death, render full satisfaction to the requirements of divine justice, and, thus representing the guilty human race, effect a full deliverance for it. This is the orthodox theory of the atonement. With minor modifications it has ever since been the view held by the evangelical church. "From the time of Anselm two opposing views of redemption were developed; the one viewed its method as objectively necessary, and derived its efficiency from this necessity; the other assigned rather a subjective connection to the two, as if it had been merely the pleasure of God to connect the price of redemption with the sufferings of Christ, because they were best adapted to effect the moral transformation of man."[91]

The argument of Anselm is based upon the recognition of the divine necessity, not to forgive, but to forgive in a way, which shows that God is irreconcilable to evil, and can never treat it as other or less than it is. And it is the recognition of this divine necessity, or the failure to recognize it, which ultimately divides interpreters of Christianity into evangelical and non-evangelical, those who are true to the New Testament and those who cannot receive it. In the *Cur Deus Homo*, where Anselm has unfolded the evangelical view, Professor Denny rightly says Christendom has the "truest and greatest book on the atonement that has ever been written."

One of these opposing views is that called the *governmental* theory. It is based upon the absolute sovereignty of God. That He, by virtue of His supreme will alone, can freely and entirely remit the guilt and penalty of sin. The right to relax the law's demands at will belongs to His prerogative as moral governor. But lest this encourage the sinner to transgress with impunity, Christ is allowed to suffer as a warning that sin shall not escape.

Another is the *moral* theory of the atonement. This is, that the sufferings of Christ on the cross were simply a transcendental display of divine love. That Christ by His death made so complete and effectual a display of God's surpassing love for sinners that their hearts are thereby melted and they are moved to forsake their sins. This moral influence theory was first propounded by the rationalistic thinker Abelard, later by the Unitarian Socinus, then by Frederick D. Maurice, and, in America, by Horace Bushnell, in his "Vicarious Sacrifice." It is the most widespread of all the views diverging from orthodoxy, and is that one probably in general acceptance in current circles of liberal thought.

The cardinal defect of these theories is that neither one makes any pretense to find support in Scripture. The governmental theory is similar to the Mohammedan conception of the divine arbitrary sovereignty, where God can pardon whom He will and on whatever grounds, and hence there would be no need of an atonement. "It therefore constituted a great advance in Latin theology, as also an evidence of its immeasurable superiority over

---

[91] Neander, History of Dogmas, p. 521.

Mohammedanism, when Anselm for the first time, in a clear and emphatic manner, had asserted an inward necessity in the being of God that His justice should receive satisfaction for the affront which had been offered to it by human sinfulness."[92]

The moral influence theory is even more objectionable. In advocating it, Horace Bushnell, in his Cambridge address on "God in Christ," objects to "the double ignominy, first, of letting the guilty go, and, secondly, of accepting the suffering of innocence." Both these theories, then, reject all idea of satisfaction; in no real sense regard Christ as a vicarious offering for sin; look upon the cross as merely a moving spectacular drama; and altogether contravene the cumulative Scriptural teaching. Nor are they legitimately entitled to be styled theories of the atonement. Rather should they be designated schemes by which to minimize and evade the atonement. In fact, a feature of our day is the use of this word theory as a plausible cover for emptying a Christian doctrine of its core and substance.

Others again, after the Ritschlian manner, oppose holding any theories of the atonement, on the ground that it is practical and not theoretical. It is argued that by this means this and other doctrines are deprived of their Scriptural simplicity and vital force. But Forrest shows that the purpose of "the Church, in proceeding carefully to define and give explicit statement to its doctrines, was not speculative but declaratory. Its aim was to conserve, not to give a theological form to the content of faith." It was compelled to do this through the vigorous assaults made upon the doctrines. They had then to be defined in such careful, intelligent, and systematic form that they could withstand attack. A theory is only a rational explanation of a thing. If we believe a Christian truth, we must believe it rationally, and be able to give an intelligent explanation of the manner in which we hold it. That is, we must have a theory of it.

Wise men seek to go to the bottom of all questions, for they know that only this is really practical. The chief cry against "theory," "theology," "philosophy," and so on, is often a veritable assertion of the all-sufficiency of shallowness in all important problems of religion and society. If as Christians we believe in a real atonement, we will have no difficulty in framing a very simple,

---

[92] Life of Jonathan Edwards — Allen, p. 88.

definite theory of it in our minds. We will take the Gospel facts and see how they accord with the law, satisfy the divine justice, and at the same time relieve the dilemma of the sinner. And our clearly defined theory will greatly strengthen and buttress our faith.

CHAPTER XV

OBJECTIONS TO THE ATONEMENT. IS GUILT TRANSFERABLE? ETHICS AND SCIENCE

IT is remarkable that the very feature of the divine redemptive scheme which commends it most forcefully to many as peculiarly displaying the love, the wisdom, and the glory of God should make it the most offensive to others. So that no teaching of the Gospel has evoked such intense antagonism and such bitter hostility, sometimes allied to contempt, as the vicarious feature of the atonement.

These objections may be classed under three heads.

1. ETHICAL

It is claimed that the vicarious principle is immoral. That to have the innocent suffer for the guilty inverts the moral poles of the universe. That to allow the guilty to escape, and the punishment to fall upon the righteous, encourages the transgressor to sin with impunity, and remits that penalty which is at once an educational and reformatory necessity for him. On this line Horace Bushnell writes on the vicarious sacrifice: "No governmental reasons can Justify even the admission of innocence into a participation of frowns and penal distributions. The eternal, unmitigable distinction between innocence and sin makes it impossible to suffer any commutation, or any the least substitution of places between the righteous and the guilty." So Martineau, contending that moral accountability is a something that cannot be shifted from one to another, says: "The transference of guilt from one individual to another, standing on the same plane, involves a contradiction of the first principle of morals."[93]

Yet plausible and weighty as these reasonings appear, they arise from a hasty and superficial view. For they fail to reflect upon and look into the deeper ethical facts that lie at the heart of things. They overlook the fact that the unity of the human race is moral as well as natural. Hence it is often a most difficult thing to draw precisely the lines which define our personal responsibility for guilt. Individual moral action is a resultant of many influences. In any particular sin the guilt is often not so much our own as that of an ancestor, who, yielding to the temptation, acquired an habitual bent or strain which was bequeathed to us. Original sin is wholly not our own, and yet it is the primal source of all our sins. The sins of the fathers visit themselves upon the children through the door of heredity. Not alone is this a Biblical truth, but it had a profound illustration in that doctrine of fate among the Greeks, portrayed with so much dramatic power in the *Œdipus Tyrannus* of Sophocles, the finest tragedy of antiquity. This conception was that the sin of some ancestor, of which the descendant was entirely ignorant, followed him like an inevitable Nemesis, involving him and his family, despite every effort, in a labyrinth of helpless disasters. Thus Sophocles makes the unhappy king say:

> For thus it pleased the gods, incensed perhaps
> Against my father's house, for guilt of old.
> For as regards my life thou couldst not find
> One spot of guilt, in recompense for which
> I sinned these sins against myself and mine.

If, then, the personal and racial elements composing the temper which precipitates into sin are often so hard to separate, and if thereby the guilt of others becomes practically transferred to us, may it not, instead of being unjust, be the profoundest principle of equity, that someone else bear the responsibility and consequences of our guilt? That as we have innocently been made to suffer for the sins of others, and that as their guilty natures and deeds have been transferred to us, so One should be found, who, innocent of our sins, yet should have our guilty natures and all their baleful consequences transferred to him? Or that, as Paul puts it, as

---

[93] Theories of the Work of Jesus, p. 479.

"through one man's disobedience many were made sinners, so through the obedience of one shall many be made righteous?"[94] It is worthy of note here that "the apostle does not raise the question whether it is possible for one to assume the responsibilities of others in this way; he assumes (and the assumption is common to all the New Testament writers) that the responsibilities of sinful men have been taken on Himself by the sinless Lamb of God. This is not a theorem he is prepared to defend, it is the Gospel he has been given to preach."[95]

That there is involved here a deep insoluble mystery it were irrational to deny, but that is no reason why it may not be true. Mysteries are the hull of the most significant and precious truths. This is constantly verified in life and science, and naturally is an important characteristic of divine revelation. All that we wish to show is the superficiality of that reasoning which would summarily dismiss the idea of the transferability of guilt as unnatural, immoral, and inconceivable.

That this law enters into the ethical constitution of the world is shown by the fact that the course of nature rests upon the death of some that others may live, *i.e.*, upon this principle of substitution or transference. Writes Drummond: "There is no reproduction in plant, animal, or man which does not involve sacrifice for others. All that is moral, and social, and other-regarding has come along the line of this function. Sacrifice, moreover, as these physiological facts disclose, is not an accident nor an accompaniment of reproduction, but an inevitable part of it. It is the universal law and the universal condition of life."[96]

Passing to a higher scale, we find that the progress of history has been evolved by the law of personal sacrifice. The noblest and the best have given themselves for the good of others, and Marcus Curtius leaps full-armed into the gulf to fulfill the decree of the soothsayers that only by the sacrifice of her rarest and best could the greatness of Rome be made eternal. A Socrates drinks the fatal hemlock, a martyr to the welfare and nobler aims of the Athenian youth; and Gustavus Adolphus spills his blood on the field that Protestantism may live and religion be free. The strong perishing

---

[94] Romans v. 19.
[95] Benny, Death of Christ, p. 99.
[96] Ascent of Man, p. 190.

for the weak; the noble bearing for the ignoble; the father sacrificing to rescue the erring prodigal; the righteous suffering to save the guilty; such is the highest law we see illustrated on the stage of life. And, so far is it from being unethical, that it has called forth the finest exhibitions of virtue, been the crucible whence has issued the purest characters, and the source of the most powerful influences for unselfish living and for obedience to the law of love that have uplifted and redeemed mankind.

And shall we then deem it unethical and immoral that, in a plan emanating from the eternal throne, and breathing the ethical spirit of Deity, this great natural law of substitution—of love suffering for others, of truth sacrificed for ignorance, of innocence bearing the sins of guilt, should find place? Or, rather, is it not what might have been expected that in this highest sphere this great law of atonement should have its fullest and sublimest illustration? That in the just suffering for the unjust, the sinless One bearing the sins of the world, the holy victim cleansing the guilty by His spotless blood, we should see not a perversion of right, but the climacteric of goodness and moral excellence?

One cannot indeed be guilty instead of another. But he can bear the punishment of another's sin. He can become one with him in sympathy and mutual aid. He can stand as his representative in meeting the righteous demands of the law. The right relation to another, after it is disturbed, may be restored independently of the violator by a third person. The question is not *how* the right relation was restored, but whether it agrees again with God's sovereign will. He who delivers a debtor from imprisonment by paying his debts restores him to his right relation to his former creditors, even though the prisoner himself did not pay a farthing of the debt. Because *righteousness has reference to mutual relations*, the right is satisfied as soon as the disturbed relation is restored and the lost position recovered. *How* it was accomplished is immaterial. And this is what Jesus did. He did not Himself become guilty, but by very virtue of His sinlessness was He able to become the efficacious offering for sin.

If the atonement be immoral, then the holding of such a false ideal would have lowered and debased the morals of those persons and peoples receiving it. But will the objector contend that such has been the case? He would not dare to maintain that the doctrine of a substitutionary atonement has produced immorality wherever it has been proclaimed. He does not venture to test his charge by an appeal to history. The appeal would be fatal. For nineteen hundred years the only great moral advances of the human race have been brought about by the preaching of a substitutionary atonement. A spring is known by its waters. It is impossible that a doctrine essentially immoral should be the cause of the purest morality among men.

2. RATIONALISTIC OR SCIENTIFIC

Of this nature is the objection, that our world occupies too insignificant a place among the mighty and countless worlds of the universe for the Creator of all to stoop so low as to give His Son to die for the souls inhabiting it. That recent revelations of science have so opened up the depths of infinity and so vastly enlarged our conceptions of the boundlessness of space, that it is inconceivable that our little planet should have been singled out as the theatre for such an extraordinary scene as that of the redemption.

But, on the other hand, with all our discoveries, how little do we really know of the universe or the stellar worlds! After all, the only sure knowledge we have is of our own. And Wallace, the rival of Darwin, in a recent very able paper contends that our solar system is a stellar globe, occupying a central position in the plane of the milky way, and that "our sun is in all probability in the center of the whole material universe." And, further, that "all the evidence at our command goes to assure us that our earth *alone* in the solar system has been from its very origin adapted to be the theatre for the development of organized and intelligent life."

These facts Wallace applies to our very point as weighty arguments, refuting those who assert the irrationality and absurdity of supposing that the Creator of all this unimaginable vastness of suns and systems should have any special interest in so pitiable a creature as man. And that He should have selected this little world for the scene of the tremendous and necessarily unique sacrifice of His Son, in order to save "poor sinners from the natural consequences of their sins, is in their view a crowning absurdity too incredible to be believed by any rational being."[97]

---

[97] Man's Place in the Universe, p. 473.

When so great a scientist can make so effective a reply, we may well leave rationalistic scientists to fight out their own doubts, leaving religion and revelation to attend to their own distinctive spheres. Let us not doubt or wonder because the Almighty doeth strange and wondrous things. He with whom is "the hiding of power," who chooses "the weak things of the world to confound the things that are mighty," and whose secret laboratory "the angels desire to look into," must not surprise us if His ways are not as our ways, or His thoughts as our thoughts. "What kind of a revelation," cries Lessing, "would that be which reveals nothing?" The latest word of science is that the furthermost bounds of discovery all reach a dark profound, an abyss of mystery, a deep where further sight is lost. Why, then, should not religion have her mysteries? Said Napoleon at St. Helena, "This is what to me proves religion to be divine, that she courageously faces those mysteries which no human system can undertake to solve."

3. THEOLOGICAL

To this class belongs the objection that our doctrine represents God as making atonement to Himself, and that this is contradictory and impossible. This objection is thus graphically voiced by Channing: "Did I believe that not the least transgression, not even the first sign of the dawning mind of the child, could be remitted without an infinite expiation, I should feel myself living under a legislation unspeakably dreadful, under laws written, like Draco's, in blood; and instead of thanking the sovereign for providing an infinite substitute, I should shudder at the attributes which render such expedient necessary. Do you mean that the great God, who never changes, whose happiness is the same yesterday, today, and forever, that this eternal Being really bore the penalty of my sins, really suffered and died? Did God take into union with Himself our nature, *i.e.*, a human body and soul, and did these bear the sufferings for our sins, and through His union with these God may be said to have borne them Himself?"

But while it is admitted that there is a mystery here, yet the explanation is plainly indicated in the doctrine of the trinity of persons in the Godhead. While the Godhead is one and could make no atonement to itself, the persons are divided, and the Son can present Himself as an offering to the Father. If this be a mystery, it is no more one than is the Trinity, or the Incarnation, or any of the great Christian doctrines.

The theological objection is further urged that the sacrificial system is Jewish, and, therefore, opposed to the Christian. But Christianity is not a contrasted religion with Judaism, but a development from it. And the sacrificial system of Judaism was not to find its contradiction but its fulfillment in that one great sacrifice, who did away with those preceding it, as substance takes the place of shadow, or as the glory of the sun pales out of view the heralding morning star.

It is objected that the ethical standards of our age have outgrown so immoral a doctrine as that of our redemption by the passion of the Son of God, and that we must modify or eliminate it, or Christianity is doomed.

The reply is that the moral sentiment of our age is no more opposed to it than was the Pagan one. When the apostles set about to proclaim this doctrine they experienced this identical opposition: "We preach Christ crucified, unto the Jew a stumbling-block, and unto the Greeks foolishness; but unto them which are called, both Jews and Greeks, Christ the power of God, and the wisdom of God."[98] Paul was not alarmed at the prophecies of failure in offering to the highly cultured Pagan world a Gospel that ran so counter to current thought. But he had sounded some of the depths of the spiritual life, and he thereby knew that many things that seemed paradoxical in the scheme of grace, only were hidings of a divine wisdom, far overtopping human wisdom. So he gives this explanation of this opposition: "But the natural man receiveth not the things of the Spirit of God; for they are foolishness unto him; neither can he know them, because they are spiritually discerned."[99]

So, though a Festus declared his preaching of the cross a madness, and though to a Celsus against Origen, and to a Porphyry against Eusebius, it seemed irrational and repellent, these great Christian leaders kept right on, not modifying one whit their unpopular message, believing it not to be foolishness, but the super-rational wisdom of God; and the result vindicated both their piety and wisdom. The cross conquered.

---

[98] I Cor. i. 23, 24.
[99] I Cor. ii. 14.

But we have more advanced ethical standards now! So thought Bauer and his great co-rationalists of the eighteenth century, who in their day carried all before them, and so thought Voltaire when he predicted that in a decade Christ would be dethroned. But they and their age passed, and yet the Christian faith abides unchanged. It is to be remembered, too, that the ethical standards of our time are the product of Christianity. And if these standards are higher than in any past era, how could it be possible that that which produced them had as the deepest center and spring of its life a "moral monstrosity?" This is inconceivable. And so Christianity need not fear that those ethical standards which have grown up under the propitiatory arms of the cross, and which Professor Huxley tells us are the noblest ideals to which the race has attained, will turn against her bosom and strike her to the heart.

Even then, quite aside from the authority of revelation, no doctrine rests upon a surer ethical basis than that of redemption. It is sustained by the analogies of nature; by the crucial facts of history; by the vicarious principle woven throughout the whole social fabric; by that deep ethical law which makes sacrifice the last test of love, and which, therefore, should find its highest illustration in a divine sacrifice,—viz., that God, who is love, should Himself give the extremest instance of sacrifice for others.

CHAPTER XVI

GROSS REPRESENTATIONS OF THE ATONEMENT

IT is a current charge against this doctrine that it is capable of great abuse. And that the manner in which it is frequently set forth is coarse, jarring to good taste and offensive to dignity and reverence. That the appeals to the sufferings of Christ and the delineations of His bodily agonies, are simply a harrowing excitement of the feelings, with no beneficial or elevating result. That the tendency of the doctrine is to encourage the belief in a magical effect wrought in the soul, without any real personal change, penitence, or transformation of character.

It is contended, also, that it is presented in a form which shifts the responsibility of sin from the transgressor to another, and thus falsely relieves his conscience and offers him an escape without that remorse and sharp moral fight which are necessary to his spiritual discipline. And it is asserted, further, that these coarse representations of the atonement are revolting to persons of cultured thoughts and refined feelings, and that they are thereby repelled from the acceptance of Christianity.

Such critics call it "a theology of blood," "a religion of gore," and similar epithets. A pamphlet of this sort is before me, with these headlines: "No blood sacrifice to appease an angry Deity. Salvation by love, not by blood. All references to blood-sacrifice should be discarded from our devotional books and sacred hymns. They are relics of a barbarous and superstitious age and revolting to every intelligent man who believes that God is love."

It may be that the tenet of a vicarious sacrifice is somewhat naturally adapted to perversions and extravagances. In the mouths of weak and hypocritical men holy mysteries are apt to receive indiscrete and hurtful treatment. In the middle ages, when deep ignorance was the rule, very crass ideas of the atoning work of Christ prevailed. An ignorant and immoral priesthood accentuated this condition, and took advantage of it for selfish purposes. Especially was it claimed that the Church possessed an exclusive right to the excessive merits of Christ's sufferings, and the supposed store of His cleansing blood was bartered out as a thing of exchange for money needed to prosecute hierarchical purposes. A well-known instance of this was the irreverent and profane campaign of Tetzel, who, setting up a great red cross, decorated with the papal arms, cried out to the ignorant crowds: "This cross has as much efficacy as the blood of Christ. An indulgence issued, with its authority, can remit any sin, no matter how heinous. If I take down that cross I will close the gate of heaven, and put out the sun of grace which shines before your eyes."

But it was unnecessary for skeptics to point out the superstition and blasphemy of these utterances. Luther, hearing of them in the confessional, was shocked, and sounded the tocsin of protest, which issued in the Reformation. But such a monstrous abuse did not abate Luther's whole-hearted belief in the atoning efficacy of Christ's blood to the penitent believer.

The mystics, while a noble class of devout souls, yet, through a suppression of the reason to the emotional sense and the imaginative faculty, were disposed to visionary experiences, and hence dwelt in a one-sided way on the vicarious work of Christ. Their habit was to exaggerate His physical sufferings rather than his spiritual agony over the burden of sin, and to indulge in sensuous expressions as to the saving power of His blood. Thus Suso often uses such expressions "as the blood of Jesus, full of love," and "red like a rose," etc. So when General Booth in his addresses employs such utterances as: "Friends, Jesus shed His blood to pay the price, and He bought from God enough salvation to go around," we feel that sacred things are so coarsely handled as to wound Christians and repel thinking unbelievers.

The cross, too, as the natural and appropriate symbol of our Lord's passion, has, doubtless, at times been made an object of superstitious reverence, amounting to practical idolatry, and earnest evangelists, lacking the intelligence and spiritual insight to discern the deeper meaning of the atonement, and with judgment overbalanced by immoderate emotion, have no doubt at times preached this doctrine with a coarseness unpleasant and hurtful.

So that we may well ask: Is there not a real danger in so presenting even this central doctrine of Christianity,—the atonement itself,—affecting as it is and ought to be, as to miss the moral convictions of men, to strike a note of unreality and disgust hearers, although we are trying to win them? Feeling and sentiment have their true place in preaching; but the sentimental, the mawkish, weak, and hysterical have no place.

But suppose such injudicious methods and grotesque figures are at times resorted to? Is that a legitimate argument against the thing itself? What cause is not liable to abuse in the hands of intemperate advocates? What truth has not been perverted by champions either not able to grasp it, or employing it for self-seeking ends?

And religion from its high and holy nature is peculiarly liable to such caricatures. Especially is this the case with Christianity, for, being the expression of religion in its highest form, its tenets are more of a supernatural nature, and more likely to be misconstrued by the human reason. A notable instance is the Lord's Supper. The uniqueness and efficacy of that sacrament depend upon the supernatural character impressed upon it by Christ's words of institution. When, therefore, the Pagans observed the reverence with which the primitive Christians celebrated it, they charged them with worshiping a "Bread God," with "carrying about their God in a wafer," etc. And the doctrine of the incarnation itself was ridiculed and travestied in the most jeering terms.

No one should wonder, then, if the atonement be sometimes set forth in crass form and sensuous language, and if it furnish a favorite target for the attack of unbelievers. That is no legitimate argument against its truth, its divinity, or its power, rightly presented, to show the love and the justice of God in so vivid a manner as to bring men to salvation.

As matter of fact, the writer has not observed that many advocates of Christianity or preachers have erred greatly in the direction charged. Very seldom has he heard such statements of the atonement as have been offensive to religious taste, or as he thought would mislead and harm. Far more frequently has he been offended by those who, while professing to preach Christ crucified, as the only ransom for sin and uncleanness, yet have been so vague and evasive on this vital truth that they have in no real or adequate sense held up Jesus on the cross as the atoning Lamb of God, to whom the soul, stung to death by the serpent of sin, must look for healing, salvation, and life.

CHAPTER XVII

DID GOD SUFFER IN THE ATONEMENT?

"LIFE," writes Hamilton Wright Mabie, "is encircled by mysteries." Every investigation of science at last leads to a cause that cannot be explained, to a problem that cannot be solved, to a profound where baffled inquiry must halt. It is not strange, then, that insoluble wonders should meet us in such a sphere as the incarnation. The apostle was able to see with the ken of inspiration, yet, lost in a maze, he cries: "Without controversy great is the mystery of godliness; God was manifest in the flesh."[100] But the deepest, darkest abyss of this mystery lies at the foot of the cross. When the great luminary of day, expressing the secret bond of the natural with the spiritual, hid His face as the agonized cry of the Crucified rent the air, must not the human mind feel its powers veiled as it endeavors to interpret the scene?

And one of the profounded questions that confronts us here is: "Did *God* suffer in the work of redemption?" We say: "Christ suffered," but what do we mean by this? Do we mean that only Jesus Christ,—the man,—suffered? No, we mean that Jesus Christ,—the Son of God,—suffered. But the Son is the second person in the Trinity; the Son is God, and if He suffered then God suffered.

This brings up the question of the union of natures in the person of Christ. Were there two Christs, one a human, and the other a divine, Christ? Can we, in the acts of Jesus, or in His sufferings, or in any of His earthly conditions, draw a line between these natures, and affirm that this was done or suffered by the man, and that by the God-Christ? No, we cannot; Christ was not two persons, but one person. He was God and man, so joined in union as to constitute the God-Man.

---

[100] I Tim. iii. 16.

Theology, in investigating this mysterious union, has applied to it what it calls the *communicatio idiomatum, i.e.,* the mutual interchange of properties. "The common participation of properties, the doctrine that the properties of the divine and human natures are actually the properties of the whole person of Christ, and are exercised by Him in the unity of His person."[101] By virtue of this principle, we must say that whatever Christ did or underwent was not the act of either nature separately, but of both natures united in one person. When a miracle was performed, it was done indeed by the power of the divine nature, but the voice or hand that mediately did it was endued from the divine side with its almighty power. So when a privation or suffering was endured, the experience was made possible by the human infirmity, but the divine, through its inseparable union, shared in it. It would not be correct indeed to say that the divine *nature* suffered of itself, for as such it is perfectly happy and incapable of suffering; nor would it be proper to say that the human *nature* of itself wrought miracles, arose from the dead, etc., for of itself it is incapable of omnipotence, but by means of their union in the one resultant personality of Jesus, each shared in the properties of the other.

Thus writes the great theologian Quenstedt: "The proposition, 'God suffered,' is thus explained: As when a wound is inflicted upon the flesh of Peter, not alone the flesh of Peter is said to have been wounded, but Peter, or the person of Peter, has been truly wounded, although his soul cannot be wounded; so, when the Son of God suffers according to the flesh, the flesh or His human nature does not suffer alone, but the Son of God, or the *person of the Son of God, truly suffers,* although the divine *nature* is incapable of suffering. While, therefore, we cannot say that the divine nature sheds blood, suffers, dies, yet by means of the personal union these actions or sufferings of the human nature are so appropriated by the divine that we can say, '*God* sheds His blood, suffers, dies.'"[102]

Startling, then, as the expression seems, and unfathomable and awe-compelling as is the mystery, it is yet correct to say that God suffered in the atonement. God shared in the humiliation of Jesus. God endured the privations of the lowly Nazarene. God tabernacled with men. God was made flesh. God felt the agonies of

---

[101] The Conservative Reformation and its Theology — Krauth, P. 477.
[102] Schmidt's Dogmatics, p. 106.

the cross. God bore upon Himself, by means of the suffering flesh, the guilt of the world. And only because of this union of the divine with the human, and only because *God* "was thus made in the likeness of men, and humbled Himself, and became obedient unto death, even the death of the cross,"[103] was it that the propitiation offered was such as no mere Christ, the man, could have offered, but had so divine, infinite, and all-potent a value that it could avail as a ransom for the sin of the whole world.

Fairbairn calls attention to the fact that even God the Father was involved in the suffering of the great atoning sacrifice. He says: "Theology has no falser idea than that of the impassibility of God. If He is capable of sorrow, He is capable of suffering; and were He without the capacity for either, He would be without any feeling of the evil of sin or the misery of man. The being of evil in the universe was to His moral nature an offense and a pain, and through His pity the misery of man became His sorrow. Through the suffering of the eternal Son, He calls all men to behold the suffering it cost the eternal Father."[104]

And this is in strict harmony with Biblical teaching. When it is written: "God so loved the world that he gave his only begotten Son;"[105] "He spared not his own Son, but delivered him up for us all,"[106] such passages either signify nothing or they mean that God illustrated His love by giving up what cost Him pain, *i.e.*, by sacrifice. And what is sacrifice but suffering? "These Scriptures by necessity imply that He, the eternal *God*, had bound Himself to suffer death from men and for them."[107]

The incarnation, then, and its climax in the atonement, was an act of sacrifice in which God the Father suffered in the surrender to humiliation and death of His Son, and in which God suffered through His union with the flesh in the person of our Lord Jesus Christ. It was not mere Man who was nailed on the cross, but they "crucified the Lord of glory."[108] Well, then, may our minds be subdued in holy awe, and our hearts be moved to their deepest center, when we look at what transpired in the mission of God's

---

[103] Phil. ii. 7.
[104] The Place of Christ in Modern Theology, p. 484.
[105] John iii. 16.
[106] Romans viii. 32.
[107] Cremer, The Work of Jesus, p. 239.
[108] I Cor. ii. 8.

eternal Son to our fallen world! And shall we wonder that at the darkest depth of the scene on Calvary the sun hid his face in troubled fear?

And do we not find in this suffering on God's part, in order to effect the redemption of man from the curse of the fall, conclusive proof that this suffering was vicarious, that it was endured to release us from the penalty? Only love could have induced such sacrifice by the Deity to whom pertains infinite happiness, and where would there have been an adequate motive, except this supreme one, that it rendered that satisfaction to infinite justice without which guilt-weighted man would have been doomed to eternal death?

If, in the tragic deed that precipitated the fall, as Milton has it:

> Earth felt the wound, and nature from her seat,
> Sighing, through all her works gave signs of woe
> That all was lost,

then the divine redemptive act that restored the lost creation could not have been effected without a vibration of pain passing through the very center of the spiritual universe, *i.e.*, felt by the heart of God.

And it is when we contemplate the atonement in the light of this revelation as to what it cost a long-suffering God—who could not give up His children to irreparable loss—that we must feel the immeasurable debt of love we owe. Verily, the grateful songs of the redeemed, on the glorified Mount of Zion, as they recount the holy wonder through eternal ages, will not exhaust the theme.

CHAPTER XVIII

MODERN VIEWS OF SIN AND THE ATONEMENT

SIN and the atonement are correlatives. One affects and determines the other. They stand or fall together. Accordingly one is the measure of the other. A correct conception of sin is essential to any right understanding of the Scriptural doctrine of the atonement. A vivid sense of sin prepares for the divine necessity of a vicarious redemption. So, where the atonement is held to but lightly, there will be a correspondingly weak and inadequate estimate of sin. The naturalistic conceptions as to the origin of the universe prevalent in large circles of modern thought tend to minimize, if not destroy, the sinfulness of sin.

The theory of evolution considers sin merely a feature of man's natural development. It is a remnant in him of his brute stage, a persistence of his animal instincts. Hence it is necessary and unavoidable, an orderly step in his upward progress. Good and evil are simply parts of a great whole. All things are linked together inevitably in the chain of cause and effect. Nothing that happens, or is done, or left undone, could have been avoided. Whatever is, is right. Evil, according to this view, becomes no more than the shadow of good, and good is the flower of evil. This view radically changes the character of sin. It is not essentially immoral, and our consciences are relieved of responsibility for it.

Akin to this is the theory that sin is wholly a matter of heredity. We have derived it from our ancestors. It is the sum of the past experiences of the race, expending its force upon us. Impulses and tendencies thus derived are beyond our control. The transgressor, the criminal, the vicious, is what he is because of inherited propensities of overmastering power. The differences in conduct between the virtuous and vicious are not moral, but natural, not the result of free choice, but of necessity. As Prof. John Fiske describes it: "We do not find that evil has been interpolated into the universe from without; we find that, on the contrary, it is an indispensable part of a dramatic whole. As we survey the course of the wonderful evolution, it begins to become manifest that moral evil is simply the characteristic of the lower state of living as looked at from the higher."

Any of these naturalistic theories quite invalidates the true character and real turpitude of sin. And, of course, where such superficial views of sin are entertained, there will be no need felt of an atonement, of a divine interposition to deliver from it.

The Scripture teaching and the doctrine of the Church conceive of sin in a radically different way. It is an unnatural thing, introduced as an alien in the natural order of the universe. It mars the harmony of the creation. It is caused by the deliberate fall of man from his state of original righteousness. It is a violation of the moral faculty bestowed upon man as his divinest prerogative. It appears as a rebel against the will of the Supreme Governor. It is a blow aimed at the justice and sanctity of His throne. It, therefore, arouses His just anger. He will not tolerate it, and hurls against it His infinite curse. "The soul that sinneth, it shall die." Evil passions, hate, strife, war, sickness, sorrow, remorse, pain and death, are its inevitable wages. Aye! even an everlasting exclusion from the presence of God and the joys of heaven,—death, spiritual and eternal,—is its woeful entail.

We find, accordingly, that the purest saints and noblest personalities have felt and mourned the dreadful fact of sin in their own personal experiences. David has given expression to this agonized conviction in the unrivaled spiritual pathos of the Psalms. Paul is driven to cry out: "O wretched man that I am, who shall deliver me from the body of this death?"[109] Augustine in his Confessions bewails it in cries that uncover the lowest deeps of the human soul, and might move a conscience of stone. Says Suso, the Mystic of the Middle Ages: "Sin is a crime against nature. It despoils the image of Deity stamped upon it. It is, therefore, a disorder of the soul, for everything is at harmony only as it keeps its natural place and state. Sin is an unrest of the heart, for, as St. Augustine says, 'Thou hast made us for Thyself, and we can only

---

[109] Romans vii. 24.

find rest in Thee.' Finally, sin is a dying of the soul, for it separates from God, in which separation is death."

This message, then, of the awful reality of sin, is the one needed to counteract the misleading tendencies of much modern thought and of science, falsely so called. We need to remember that the largest, blackest fact this side of heaven is the fact of sin. Over against this awful, deadly fact, higher than the Sierras and deeper than the sea, is the mightier, more majestic fact of the grace of God in redemption. No man can understand the atonement who has not truly seen sin. No man knows the meaning of Calvary except in the lurid light of Sinai. No man can even try to measure the grace of God in his own heart except as against the awful background of sin and death and hell.

The natural mind, of course, has and can have no realistic sense of the fact of sin. The world about us goes on its course quite unconscious of the deadly malady which afflicts it. One of the worst features of the disease is the moral paralysis which prevents the victim from suspecting his condition. Hence, until the Holy Spirit has convicted the conscience, and the soul gets a new view of its relation to God and His righteous laws, an adequate conception of sin is impossible.

More than all else, then, does our age need the understanding and conviction of sin. Hence, instead of avoiding it, because distasteful and unpopular, upon its presentation rather, both in the exposition of the Scriptures and in the preaching of the Gospel, should be laid the chief emphasis.

CHAPTER XIX

THE ATONEMENT AND THE HEATHEN

IF the atonement be grounded upon an eternal divine necessity, in that God cannot overlook sin with impunity, and that He cannot be the justifier of the sinner without a just regard to the broken law, what then are we going to do with the heathen? In what sort of dilemma does this leave them, since they cannot be saved without the one all-atoning sacrifice, and yet have had no opportunity to know of it? This is a real difficulty, and a real moral bar, if valid, to the atonement. For it will not do to say that God can simply will to save the heathen, without a Mediator. For if, waiving His attribute of justice, He could do this with them, He could do it with all men. Then it was not necessary that Christ should suffer, and thus the whole redemptive scheme falls.

The difficulty, then, is one that must be met. The only solution of it is to be found in the Scriptures,—the source of all Christian belief. These teach that all have sinned, that all are under condemnation, and that all can be saved through Christ alone. "For there is none other name under heaven given among men whereby we must be saved."[110] This certainly includes the heathen, and would, if unmodified by other Scriptures, inexorably shut them out from the kingdom of God. But other passages assert the exact and equal-handed justice of God and His impartial Fatherhood to all His children, as: "God is no respecter of persons, but in every nation he that feareth Him and worketh righteousness is accepted of Him."[111] And still others declare that the will of God, to save by free grace, extends to the whole human race. How are these apparently conflicting Scriptural statements to the reconciled?

---

[110] Acts iv. 12.
[111] Acts x. 34.

This leads us to a third class of passages, which suggest the necessary bridge between the two. Of these there are three remarkable ones: one which tells how the Spirit of Christ, while His body lay in the grave, descended to Hades and "preached to the spirits in prison,"[112]—the transgressing peoples of the antediluvian world;—the second, "For this cause was the Gospel preached to them that are dead;" and the third, "which describes a tree whose leaves are for the healing of the nations," located not in time, but in eternity. To this must be added the postponement of the General Judgment to the close of time, intimating that the particular judgment at death may not, in every case, be irrevocable.

May we not here, then, find the key of this difficult problem? While the Scriptures teach that, without the atonement provided by Christ, none can be saved, yet, if in this intermediate state, the heathen should have the saving way proclaimed to them; and while the Scriptures teach that there is no second probation, yet if a first probation be thus given to those denied it in time; may we not find here a solution of the dark problem?

But is not Christian orthodoxy bound to the view of the eternal loss of the heathen? This is perhaps generally supposed, and is often regarded as the strongest motive for the prosecution of Christian missions. And the writer holds orthodoxy in the highest regard, so that he would risk not the slightest departure from the safe enclosure of the common faith of Christendom. But the Christian Fathers do not teach that it is impossible that the heathen be saved. The orthodox Chrysostom says: "The eunuch of Ethiopia God overlooked not. It is not the case that any naturally religious man ever was overlooked." Clement, of Alexandria, writes: "If the Lord descended to Hades to preach the Gospel to the prisoners, then all who believe shall be saved, as making their profession there. For it is not right that these should be condemned without trial, and that those who lived after the Advent should have the advantage."[113] Wrote the late Dr. Schaff: "The modern German Protestant opinion in its evangelical form maintains that Christ will ultimately be revealed to all human beings—that there is therefore a possibility of pardon and salvation in the state between

---

[112] I Peter iii. 20.
[113] I Peter iv. 6.

death and the resurrection for heathen and all others who die innocently ignorant of Christ."[114]

While it would be alike unwise and irreverent to dogmatize on so mysterious a problem, it may be that we here find the golden *via media*. It avoids that heretical liberalism which would teach that men can be saved by reason and the light of nature alone, thereby making needless the great scheme of the atonement, discrowning Christ and making useless Gospel missions. Equally it avoids that harsh extreme,—the doom to eternal misery of millions dying unenlightened without their own fault—a position not only repugnant to God as an ethical and paternal Being, but directly opposed to the Scriptural presentations of Him, and to the declared universality of the offer of grace. The atonement then extends to the heathen; it reaches back to those who were before Christ's day; it is coeval with time and co-extensive with the creation. It embraces to the uttermost all those who by faith seek and accept its gracious offer.

---

[114] Rev. xxii. 2.

CHAPTER XX

THE ATONEMENT AND MODERN HERESIES

As that "Jesus died for our sins according to the Scriptures" is the pivotal and all-regulative principle of New Testament truth, so it becomes the touchstone of all sound teaching and orthodox doctrine. The one who is fixed on this central truth will be evangelical to the core. It will put him at right relations with all other articles of the Christian faith. It will keep him from holding false, one-sided, and distorted views of any portion of Christian doctrine.

Contrariwise, if we examine the tenets of any sect claiming the Christian name, we can safely test its soundness or heresy by its attitude to the atonement. If its views cannot be reconciled with this fundamental article, or minimize or practically exclude it, then we may know that its system is at heart non or anti-Christian.

Rationalism is that temper which makes reason, as opposed to revelation, the seat of authority in religion. Kahnis thus characterizes it:

"In general, Rationalism is that tendency which, in matters of faith, makes reason the measure and rule of truth. It is distinguished from Theism or Naturalism chiefly by connecting its own rationalistic belief with the faith and doctrine of the Church, and by the opinion that in so doing they have laid hold of the substance of it."[115]

Rationalism is at once the most ancient as well as the most modern of heresies. In the Middle Ages, Abelard stands forth as its great representative in his querulous disputations with the saintly Bernard. In our time the higher critics largely evince its spirit. The atonement is the last discovery that could have been made by the

---

[115] History of Protestantism — Illuminism, p. 168.

human reason. Hence where it, over against revelation, is made the test of what God did, or could have done, in the work of redemption, the atonement is dismissed with curt tolerance. The identical canons of investigation which the Rationalists applied to the Faith and its theology, the higher critics apply to their analysis of the Scriptures—the Rule of Faith. And just as Kahnis shows how, when "Rationalism stood in the pulpit a victor, the churches were emptied," so disastrous to practical Christianity and the Church would be the victory of these champions of modern Rationalism.

Thus with *Universalism*. Placing undue emphasis on the love of God, so as to ignore the legitimate sphere of His attribute of justice, there is no wrath from which the sinner needs to be delivered, and hence no occasion for a vicarious Redeemer.

Unitarianism, which though a small body, yet exerts so large a religious influence, owing to the intelligence and high character of its advocates, does not claim to be orthodox, but rejoices in what it deems the freedom of its liberal thought from the fetters of traditional and historical belief. Denying, as it does, the true divinity of Christ, however else it may do Him homage, it must deny the atonement, for, if Christ be but man, how can He be a propitiation for the sins of men any more than they could be such for themselves? Accordingly, one of the ablest and noblest-minded of this sect, Martineau, writes: "The apostle in his statement, 'Him that knew no sin, God made to be sin for us, that we might be made the righteousness of God in Him,"[116] means that through the cross and resurrection there is a change of places between us and Christ; He taking our penalty, and we becoming invested with His righteousness. That the apostle did not shrink from this conception of vicarious sin and retribution seems strange to us, schooled as we are in individualism and lonely responsibility...The mythology of redemption here assumed its most consistent and intelligible shape. The subsequent change in the medieval period, resolving the whole transaction into a juggle between conflicting attributes of the infinite Perfection, did but replace a childish forensic fiction by a monstrous moral enormity."[117] No more positive and peremptory rejection of the atonement could be found than in

---

[116] 2 Cor. iii. 9.
[117] Seat of Authority in Religion, pp. 479 and 485.

these strong words. Our Unitarian friends certainly do not regard Christ as the Savior in the same sense in which we do.

The strangest of heresies is the irrational delusion which assumes the appellative, *Christian Science*. It starts with the denial of sin. Writes its founder, Mrs. Eddy: "Soul cannot sin. Man is incapable of sin, sickness, or death,"[118] thus directly denying Scripture, which declares: "The soul that sinneth, it shall die," and "The wages of sin is death."[119] The next step in this fallacious argument is strictly logical. If there be no sin, there can be no sense of guilt. So the founder of this cult writes further: "You had better be exposed to every plague on earth than to endure the cumulative effects of a guilty conscience. The abiding consciousness of wrong-doing tends to destroy the ability to do right."[120] According to this we are to silence those protests of conscience, to refuse those penitential contritions, and to hush that sense of moral accountability, which the Word of God ever seeks to arouse and quicken in us, as a "godly sorrow that worketh a repentance unto salvation not to be repented of."[121]

Further, no one is in any danger of divine punishment: "In common justice we must admit that God will not punish man for doing what He created him capable of doing."[122] Certainly, if as we are here taught, there be no sin, no sense of guilt, and no punishment to be averted, then there can be no need of or place for a Savior, and the whole scheme of the atonement falls to the ground. So we are not surprised to read from the same authoress: "Deliverance from error is not reached by pinning one's faith to another's vicarious effort."[123] Again, we are oracularly told that "the material blood of Jesus was no more efficacious to cleanse from sin when it was shed on the accursed tree, than when it was flowing in His veins as He went daily about His Father's business." It is doubtful if Christ suffered at all, though nailed on the cross; and if He did suffer, the cause assigned for it is one altogether out of the natural order of cause and effect, as it is also divorced from the logical process of thought. According to Mrs. Eddy it is this: "If

---

[118] Science and Health, p. 464.
[119] Rom. VI.23.
[120] Science and Health, p. 402.
[121] 2 Cor. vii. 10.
[122] Science and Health, p. 302.
[123] Ibid., p. 427.

Jesus suffered, it must have been through the mentality of others."
Surely here we have an illustration of the errorist whom the
apostle rebukes as one "who hath trodden under foot the Son of
God, and hath counted the blood of the covenant wherewith he
was sanctified an unholy thing, and hath done despite unto the
spirit of grace."[124]

Modern *Theosophy*, a heathen importation from India, a
reproduction of the heresy of gnosticism which Paul and the
Primitive Christian Fathers found a dangerous enemy, likewise
denies the atonement. Its chief exponent in this country, from
whom Mrs. Eddy has drawn the leading articles of her system,
often copying her very words, writes: "A vicarious actor, whether
God or man, is most revolting and most degrading to human
dignity." Again, "That is a dangerous doctrine which teaches that
if we have committed trespasses against the laws of God and of
man, no matter how enormous, we have but to believe in the self-
sacrifice of Jesus for the salvation of mankind, and His blood will
wash out every stain."

We observe here the similarity of method employed by modern
and ancient paganism, viz., misrepresentation and ridicule.
Christianity, all know, demands repentance, purity, and spiritual
renewal as the concomitant of faith. A mere mental faith, such as
is here described, without regeneration of heart and holiness of life,
is a caricature of the faith insisted on in the Gospel. It is that which
the New Testament repudiates in the expressive phrase: "The
devils believe and tremble."

Theosophy makes very large pretensions. It claims to teach the
generic truth of all religions, and invites those of any religious faith
whatever to take shelter under its ample folds. Its tolerance is great
enough to shelter all forms of religious error. Knowing nothing of
justification by faith, preaching a salvation by works, and
welcoming all manner of views, it is one of the subtlest foes of
Christianity.

Such travesties of the truth show into what dangerous heresies
those fall, who let go their hold upon that great trunk of the
Christian tree—the atonement, which upholds all the branches and
binds them together. And by this test can the plainest Christian
detect any one of these flagrant heresies which so abound in our

---

[124] Heb. x. 29.

day and which are a temptation and a snare, leading the souls of the simple and unwary to "perdition and destruction." Of any would-be teacher who is unsettled and gives an uncertain sound on this fundamental point, we must beware. For such a one utterly misconceives the Gospel and deranges its whole structure. He has no adequate conception of Christianity. And if he professes to have built up a system, it is not only non, but positively anti-Christian. For whoever uses the name of Christ to give authority to a cult that offers righteousness and salvation in any other way than that of the one all-atoning sacrifice is guilty of the denial of Christ and of the attempt to rob Him of His redemptive crown.

That an age should be so prolific in heresies as is ours should not distress or alarm us. For the times of the hottest controversy with the enemies of truth have always been the richest for the gain of positive truth in the Christian confession. The central doctrines of the faith have obtained their definite form and their clearest brightness in the fiery crucible of assault and defense. "The King has cast His Church into the midst of warfare and trouble; He has not permitted it to confess His name in an unmanly and indolent manner, but from age to age He has compelled it to defend that confession against error, misunderstanding, and hostility. It is only in this warfare that it has learned, gradually, to exhibit every part of its glorious inheritance of truth. God shall judge heretics; but, besides much mischief, they have rendered the Church this excellent service of compelling it to wake up from slumbering upon its gold-mines, to explore them, and to open the hidden treasure."

The apotheosis of heresy is a characteristic of the present. We often hear the remark, and many receive it as an approved fact: "The heretics of yesterday are the orthodox leaders of today." No falser apothegm was ever uttered. A résumé of the whole field of history presents its constant and emphatic refutation.

Were the conspicuous heretics of the past, such as Celsus, Pelagius, Arius, Abelard, Carlstadt, and Socinus, to return in the flesh, they would find their names forgotten, or recorded but as a beacon of warning.

Whereas the names of those who respectively contended against these arch-heretics, Origen, Augustine, Athanasius, St. Bernard, Luther and Calvin are only brightening with lapsing time; their memories are increasingly venerated; and from their immemorial thrones they are still formulating the theology and molding the faith and conduct, and swaying the destinies of our modern age.

And could these great orthodox leaders reappear, theologians and materialists, kings and thinkers, the heads of the Church, and the masses of the people, would rise up to give them an ovation of welcome such as this world has never witnessed.

CHAPTER XXI

THE NEGATIVE HIGHER CRITICISM AND THE ATONEMENT

CHARACTERISTIC of our day is the activity, dogmatism, and predominance in large circles of what is called the higher criticism. This is the critical analysis of the origin, date, authorship, canonicity, contents, etc., of the books of the Bible. It is determined largely by subjective conceptions based upon internal evidence. It is called higher as distinct from lower, which has to do with fixing the pure, original text of Scriptures.

Legitimately the higher criticism has nothing to do with the character of Scriptural doctrines. How then has it any bearing on the tenet of the atonement? It should have none. Yet the point that concerns us is that, whether logically or not, the higher criticism authorities and those who defer to them are inclined to take a low view of the sacrificial death of Christ, if not to discountenance it altogether. No article of our Christian faith seems more to incite their antagonism.

As illustrative of this, let us cite a few representative witnesses. One of the foremost of the higher critics, Cheyne, says: "There is no doctrine of the sacrifice of Christ in the New Testament, as there may be said to be doctrines of redemption or justification. In describing the death of Christ as a sacrifice, the New Testament writers are using figurative language. Some modern theologians, indeed, still affirm that the apostles held it to be a sacrifice in the literal sense, but such writers do not expect us to take their literal literally."[125]

Harnack expresses himself thus: "Now if we were to consider the conception attaching to the words 'expiatory death' in the alien realm of speculation, we should soon find ourselves in a blind alley.

---

[125] Encyclopedia Biblica, p. 4232.

We should be absolutely at the end of our tether, if we were to indulge in speculating as to the necessity which can have compelled God to require such a sacrificial death. No reflection of the reason will ever be able to expunge from the moral ideas of mankind the conviction that injustice and sin deserve to be punished, and that everywhere that the just man suffers, an atonement is made which puts us to shame and purifies us."[126] It is evident that the atonement here viewed is simply such a one as all good men make when they die for a righteous cause. But there is a bridgeless chasm between the atonement which we make for another and that which Christ made for us.

Ritschl is much bolder: "It need not be said that he rejects absolutely the ordinary satisfaction theory of the death of Christ. There are no premises in his system from which such a theory, or any modification of it, could be deduced. There is no principle in the character of God demanding punishment for its own sake; no wrath of God against sin; no objective condemnation resting on the race—the Pauline κατάκριμα—from which, as a first step in his salvation, the sinner needs deliverance. The sole obstacle to his reconciliation is his own guilt-consciousness and the distrust of God which this engenders. For the removal of this is needed no such atonement for sins as the ordinary theory supposes, but only the revelation of the forgiving grace of God."[127]

As an evidence of the current attitude of those who accept the extreme results of modern Biblical criticism, we may take the following from a late editorial in the *New York Independent:*

"Christ *died on the cross.* This is a very important fact and very useful to Christianity, and yet Christianity would exist if Christ had ascended without dying. God would still have been a loving Father, and could have forgiven prodigals just the same. Christianity does not require us to look on the death of Christ as propitiating the Father, who needs nobody to excite or encourage His love. No expiatory sacrifice is needed, for God is abundantly able to forgive, out of His own store of love. Christ's death is the crown of His life, teaching, and example. It proves His genuineness and is a power to draw us into a life like His; but it is not an expiatory sacrifice."

---

[126] What is Christianity ? pp. 156-159.
[127] Orr on the Ritschlian Theology, p. 149.

These citations have an instructive significance. The alleged aims of the teachers and advocates of the higher criticism are to conserve the Scriptures, and to add to their authority by shedding light and intelligibility upon them. Yet here we find them employing their instruments of scientific criticism to impair and even quite invalidate the central fact and doctrine of the New Testament.

"Their treatment of the Old Testament makes a revolution in Hebrew history. Abraham was a mythical figure. Moses wrote no laws nor history; David wrote no psalms; Solomon no proverbs. The pillar of fire did not precede the journeying Israelite. The Lord did not command the construction of a tabernacle. There is no trace of sin and guilt offerings in the Old Testament before Ezekiel. The divine and supernatural is eliminated according to the radical school of critics. If these things be so, it follows that the promise and doctrine of redemption are not the substance, and the sole reason of existence for the Old Testament."[128]

Is not the conclusion just that a system which reaches such destructive results is characterized by a false internal principle? Either that its aims are destitute of that faith and reverence which are essential to a safe Biblical critic? Or that its methods are unscientific and unreliable? In either case, the destructive crucible in which the higher criticism casts so precious and vital a Christian article as that of the atonement is sufficient to put the believer carefully on his guard in accepting many of its rash hypotheses and unwarranted conclusions.

---

[128] The Higher Criticism, Dr. T. E. Schmauk, p.11.

CHAPTER XXII

THE ATONEMENT AND CHRISTIAN HISTORY

WE live in an age which discountenances authority. Liberty and progress are its watchwords. The tendency is to idolize the present and to slight the past as effete and exploded. The old is worthless; the new is the horizon that glows with promise, truth and life. We must break away from the fetters of authority, and bask in a freedom with no limits but those of capricious individualism. But, while this is the cry on so many lips, it does not represent those deeper thinkers who, after all, conserve and mold the world's progress. They recognize it as but superficial, unwise and unsafe. They know that there is a moral unity in the ages, and that the individual thought of one time must align itself with the universal thought of all times. Past, present, and future must all bear their part in that belief, in that consciousness, in that thought, in that conclusion, which is the right and final one. The true is the universal; the universal alone is the eternal. As Ruskin puts it, "Men are not working as isolated units, independent of each other's efforts, but the successive generations all together are rolling one mighty, ever-gathering snow-ball up the Alpine heights of mental power."

Hence it is not the conception which any one religious teacher or spiritual genius has of a Scriptural doctrine which, as a rule, is the reliable one, but that interpretation reached by the common Christian sense—that doctrine affirmed by the Christian consensus of all times—that which bears the imprint of universal Christendom. This test of universality, like all principles, is subject to misconception and abuse, but it still remains the most judicious and safe for human guidance. The formula of Vincent, *Quod semper, quod ubique, quod ab omnibus creditum est*—"That which has been believed always, everywhere, and by all"—although often perverted to prop up outworn error and to defend spiritual tyranny, yet can never lose its genuine application and its commanding influence with sensible men. We must think for ourselves; but he is a rash thinker, and will soon wander in misleading fallacies, who will not temper his single judgment by the accordant judgment of millions in diverse ages.

Now, if this axiom have application anywhere, it is to the atonement. Upon no other article of Christianity has there been such a constant and unanimous agreement. Apostolic, Medieval, and Modern Christendom, the Eastern, the Roman, and the Protestant Church here are all one. Scarcely, indeed, have any heresies within the Church arisen with respect to it as about other Christian doctrines.

A resume of Christian opinion makes this manifest.

Of the apostolical fathers, Clement, the co-laborer of St. Paul, whose name he tells us (Phil. 4:3) "is in the book of life," writes: "Christ bore our iniquities and suffered for our sakes. He was wounded for our transgressions and bruised for our sins."[129] Ignatius (A.D. 70)—"Jesus Christ died for us, in order that, by believing in His death, we might be made partakers in His resurrection."[130] Justin Martyr (A.D. 130)—"Christ endured the passion of the cross, cleansing by His blood those who believe in Him. For this blood was not of human seed, but of divine power."[131] Irenæus (A.D. 160)—"The death of Christ was the crown of His redemptive work."

The great representative fathers of the Greek and Latin Primitive Churches write respectively: Chrysostom (380 A.D.)—"There is but one sacrifice. The blood of Christ has cleansed all men. This blood flowed not, as in the Old Testament, from the bodies of irrational animals, but from the body of Christ, prepared by the Spirit."[132] Augustine (400 A.D.)—"Christ assumed our flesh that He might offer a sacrifice for our justification. Death itself, although the punishment of sin, was submitted to by Him for our sakes, who was without sin. For He was able to expiate our sins by

---

[129] First Epistle of Clement, chapter xvi.
[130] Epistle to the Trollians, chapter ii.
[131] First Apology, chapter xxxii.
[132] Homilies on Hebrews,

dying for us."[133] In the Middle Ages, Suso, representing the mystics, who bathed so deeply in the ocean of divine love, writes: "Lord Jesus, I will deserve Thy paradise, not through any merits of my own, but through the power of Thy blessed passion, by which Thou dost redeem me, a poor sinner, at the price of Thy precious blood."

And so on down through the Reformation and to this modern age. Not a note of dissent is to be heard in the universal diapason of the Christian witness. The atonement is so shot through the whole Christian system that it could not be eliminated without the latter falling to pieces. It is the cornerstone of every Evangelical Confession. It forms the fiber of all the historic liturgies. It is the sweetest and richest theme running through our hymnology. In short, to eradicate it would require so radical a revolution and so destructive a process that the beating heart of Christianity would be removed and nothing left but its lifeless corpse.

To the unanimity of the testimony let us cite a few representative historical authors: Hagenbach—"From the very beginning, on the basis of Apostolic Christianity, the redeeming element was put chiefly in the sufferings and death of Christ. The first teachers of the Church regarded this death as a sacrifice and ransom, and, therefore, ascribed to the blood of Jesus the power of cleansing from sin and guilt."[134] Hodge—"It is no less certain that the whole Christian world has ever regarded the sacrifice for sin to be expiatory. Such is the faith of the Latin, of the Lutheran, and of the Reformed Churches, all the great historical bodies which make up the sum of professing Christians; such is the world-wide belief, the concurrent judgment of the Christian Church in all ages and places."[135] Jackson—"The common church doctrine, although so often and severely assailed, is sustained by the sacrificial system of the Old Testament, by the express teachings of our Lord and His apostles, by the moral nature of man, and by the experience of believers of all ages."[136] And even Harnack, in spite of his prepossessions, is constrained to admit: "The ideas which from the beginning onward have been roused by Christ's death, and have,

---

[133] City of God, chapter xxv.
[134] History of Doctrines, vol. i., p. 179.
[135] Systematic Theology, vol. ii., p. 500.
[136] Dictionary of Religious Knowledge, p. 62.

as it were, played around it, leave no reason to doubt the fact how the death and the shame of the cross came to take the central place."[137]

Yet the claim has been put forth that the doctrine of a vicarious atonement is a "changeling," appearing at a later date as a substitute for the primitive belief. And the ground alleged for this is that the Scriptural facts were first marshalled into a definite theory by Anselm. But, in reaching this precise definition, it simply followed the natural processes of thought. None of the great doctrines of the Church appeared at once in theological form. They lay like loose stones in the quarry, not as yet cut and fitted into the edifice. Even the Deity of Christ was not formally defined until the time of the Nicene symbol, while the articles on Justification by Faith and the Person of Christ were only theologically stated as late as the Reformation era.

But how groundless to hold that these essential doctrines were not received and confessed during all the foregoing time! The fact is that they were universally held during the preceding ages. It was only when there arose some to question them that, for an apologetic purpose, Christian thinkers found it desirable to give them logical statement, according to the necessary laws of thought. Therefore, they were set in a theological system and correlated with the other Christian doctrines, so as to form a scientific unity. To style this a change of substance is as incorrect as to say that gold taken from the mine, minted and stamped, is no longer identical with the mineral in its rough state of ore. The assumption that the formulation of Scripture doctrines into a logical system is a repudiation of them, would end all building upon the foundation of truth, would make a scientific theology impossible, and would forever fix the Christian doctrines in a Procrustean form, just as they were announced nineteen centuries ago. This would be the stiffest anti-progressive conservatism conceivable.

Never, then, has the Church changed as to the doctrine of the vicarious atonement. Practically it is that one doctrine as to which there has been unbroken unanimity. The Christian writings of all ages are steeped in it. All have felt its denial tantamount to an abandonment of the integral principle of Christianity.

---

[137] What is Christianity ? p. 160.

Such an unbroken verdict of Christian history as this is not likely to be discarded. It cannot but have a convincing force for the believer. If all the Christian world has believed in a substitutionary atonement; if the first century and the twentieth century agree in this; if all the historic creeds, liturgies, prayers, and hymns are based upon it; if the great historic systems of theology enshrine it as the very Ark of the Covenant, as the Holy of Holies; is it not chimerical to regard it as a delusion and an error? Is it not rather the rational conclusion that all these interpretations are the true one, and that the only solution of this united testimony of the ages is that the orthodox theory of the atonement is so plainly and irresistibly set forth in the Scriptures that he who runs must read in it God s plan for saving the world?

CHAPTER XXIII

THE LUTHERAN VIEW OF THE ATONEMENT

THIS treatise has been prepared with no denominational interest. It is written in defense of our common Christianity. Happily, on the essential tenets of our faith, the evangelical denominations are at one. The primary truths we all receive; those that divide us are secondary. And while, as Lessing says, "the smallest particle of truth is God-given and possesses an infinite value," still our differences on relatively minor aspects of doctrine are insignificant as compared with our unity on the great fundamentals. And in this day, when the very citadel of the faith is assailed on so many sides, and so many professed friends are found to be weakening, the great evangelical denominations should feel more closely drawn together than ever by their unity in the cardinal principles of their belief. And from the preeminence held by the atonement, it is natural that on it, even more than on any other article, there should be manifest this mutual agreement. So it is matter of profound congratulation that in respect to this doctrine the leading Christian Churches stand together with largely unbroken front.

Yet, as the author is one of its office-bearers, it is proper that he should bear witness as to the position on this question of the Evangelical Lutheran Church. Its attitude here is remarkably unshaken, positive, and clear. There are several features in its doctrinal character which contribute to this even in an exceptionable degree.

One of these is the clearly defined attitude of the Lutheran Church to the *Scriptures*. It holds unwaveringly to them as the record of a genuine revelation, believing that they were given through a supernatural inspiration, and hence have absolute authority as the only infallible rule of faith and practice. Hence the Scriptural teachings are not to be explained according to the subjective views of the reader, but to be taken in their natural, grammatical, evident sense. But, as the Scriptures everywhere so pre-eminently set forth the sacrificial plan of man's redemption, the Church that does not, in the face of the fierce assault upon them, compromise her loyalty in the least to their authority, cannot either weaken her stand on this point as to their testimony.

Again, the Lutheran Church places special emphasis on the fact of *sin*. It was the bitter experience of it in his soul, as alienating from God, rendering morally helpless, and incurring eternal penalty, which drove Luther in the cloister to find his deliverance alone in an infinite remedy. Where sin is realized in its full enormity, and is not minimized and evaded by any theory of easy-going modern Pelagian sentiment, there special stress must be laid upon the necessity of the divine plan of atonement. Thus writes Gerhard, that prince of Lutheran theologians: "It was the infinite God that was offended by sin; and because sin is an offense, wrong, and crime against the infinite God, and, so to speak, is Deicide, it has an infinite evil, and deserves infinite punishment, and, therefore, required an infinite price of satisfaction, which Christ alone could have afforded."[138]

Further, the Lutheran Church elevates to the first place in the divine perfections the attribute of *Love*. Love with her is the key that unlocks the mysteries of the Scriptures, and sheds light upon the dark, strange problems of life and Providence. The love of God is the corner-stone and constructive principle of her theology. It is the prominence given this attribute in the divine perfections which explains the hearty joyousness, and the sunny, genial type of piety which characterize the Lutheran peoples of all lands. And as no article in the Christian faith so displays the love of God and so intensely reveals the glory of the divine tenderness and compassion as does the cross, with its blood-and-agony-purchased redemption, so does the atonement peculiarly harmonize with the spirit of this Church.

Again, the Lutheran Church is *Christo-centric*. The Scriptures, for her pre-eminently, testify of Christ. They are to be explained in the light of His incarnation. The keystone of the Word is that it

---

[138] III., 579. Schmid's Doctrinal Theology of the Lutheran Church, p. 374.

sets forth Christ, finds its fulfillment in Him, bears the imprint of His spirit. Lutheran theology is built upon the God-Man. He is the central Sun about which it revolves. The theologians of the Lutheran Church have meditated most deeply over questions of Christology. Perhaps the most notable contribution to theology since the Reformation era has been made by Lutheran thinkers in the development of the doctrine of the Person of Christ. God in Christ, in the Lutheran Church, is the beginning, middle, and end of theology.

And once more, with the Lutheran Church, the chief Christian article is that of *Justification by Faith*. This is the all-regulative, determining principle. Every other article of Christian doctrine in her theological system must be tested and adjusted by it.

The doctrines of the Word of God form an harmonious whole. They are all parts which, fitted together, constitute one great unity. Their full and accurate statement issues in a perfect system of truth. And as the chief pillar in this edifice of Christian doctrine is that of justification by faith, so no interpretation of Scripture can be true which conflicts with it.

Luther thus called the Article of Justification "the master, the prince, the lord, the ruler, the judge over all kinds of doctrine," which governs all the doctrine of the Church. "This is the most important article of Christian faith. When this knowledge of justification is lost, at the same time Christ and life and the Church are lost."[139]

No good works of our own, no bitterness of repentance, no agonizing emotional struggles justify the sinner; but solely the atoning merits of Christ, given on condition of faith alone. This faith is the gift of God to those who do not resist the movings of the Holy Spirit, but open their hearts to the Means of Grace. But if salvation is thus not merely of God's sovereign pleasure, irrespective of the satisfaction due to His broken law and offended justice, nor of any works of righteousness which we have done, but by faith alone in the crucified One, then surely Christ must have paid the whole debt, then His blood must wash every stain of guilt away, then there must have been a truly vicarious atonement.

Such are distinguishing traits of the Lutheran Church which tend to give the atonement a high place in her theology, in her

---

[139] Koestlin, Theology of Luther, vol. ii., p. 212.

affections, and in its regulative power in her Christian life. Thus says the Augsburg Confession: "Christ truly suffered and was crucified that He might reconcile the Father to us and be a sacrifice, not only for original sin, but also for all actual sins of men;" and the Form of Concord completes the statement: "So that on account of this complete obedience, which by deed and in suffering, in life and in death, He rendered His heavenly Father for us, God forgives our sins, regards us godly and righteous, and eternally loves us."[140]

While, as we have said, the other denominations, as such, still hold to the atonement, yet it is to be deplored that in many quarters the tendency of current Christian thought is to a dangerous weakening on this vital point. In the recent volume of Dr. Karl Hermann Wirth on "The Doctrine of Merit in the Christian Church," he truly says: "The doctrine of human merit is one which, even today, is not only of most far-reaching importance for the Roman church, but also rules, or at least dims, the views of numerous evangelical Christians." And, because the Lutheran Church has so absolutely rejected human merit, and ascribed all merit to the atonement, laying its chief emphasis, on man's side, on justification by faith alone, she has been charged with indifference to immorality and holiness, "letting her adherents go to heaven on flowery beds of ease." But she can well bear these misrepresentations in the consciousness of her pure confession of this vital truth of the Gospel.

And it is certainly cause for rejoicing and assurance that, whatever misgivings and uncertainties may disturb other evangelical communions respecting changing views in regard to the atonement, there are none such in the Mother Church of the Reformation—the one universally distributed over the globe, teaching the Gospel in all languages, and numbering 70,000,000 members, a number, perhaps, equal to that of all other Protestants combined.

Not only are her confessions and her theology evangelical on the atonement, but her pulpits likewise. No mere ethical preaching, no gospel of moral reform or self-help, is heard from any of her ministers. Not the approval of the spirit of the age, not the applause of the light literature of the time, not worldly popularity and numbers do her pulpits seek after; but conversions, new-born

---

[140] Jacobs's Lutheran Confessions, p. 572.

souls, smitten consciences led from sin to righteousness and from death to life; and so she holds up Jesus on the cross, and, through faith in Him alone, justification unto life.

CHAPTER XXIV

THE SINNER'S JUSTIFICATION BY FAITH

ALLUSION in general terms has often been made in the foregoing chapters—and especially in the preceding one—to Justification by Faith. This term—justification—holds so integral a place in the Scriptural presentation of the Atonement as to demand a special treatment in any thorough consideration of the doctrine.

The first step in the sinner's reconciliation to God—to be followed by his inner, growing, personal renewal—is his justification. He must be held juridically righteous. There must be a readjustment of his moral relations to the righteous Judge. He must appear before God, no longer as dyed in sin and guilt, but as cleansed, as having his iniquities covered, as clothed in the wedding robe of spotless righteousness. Only when he occupies this position, when he can be regarded as a cleansed moral creature, can God have ought to do with him, recognize him as His child, and can the recreative spiritual process go forward in him in all its freedom, fullness, and power.

And the Scripture further teaches that this justification is all of divine grace, not of human works. No moral effort of man, no self-reformation, no agonizing penitential experiences, no force or power of self-determination can effect it. Left to himself and his best efforts, man can never be anything but an alien from, and an enemy to, his God. For the Holy One is of purer eyes than to behold iniquity, and, do the most he can, the sinner will still stand amenable to the curse of the broken law.

But in this helpless dilemma the Son of God meets the exigency. He presents Himself in the sinner's stead, and renders up a sacrifice of all-availing power. He offers a full and perfect atonement for his sins, no matter how manifold, grievous, and inexcusable: "And the blood of Jesus Christ, his Son, cleanseth us from all sin." "While we were yet sinners, Christ died for us."

But while the provision is thus amply made by the gracious goodness of God, how shall the guilt-burdened sinner avail himself of the remedy? How shall he apply to himself the healing grace? How shall the righteousness of Jesus be made his own? How shall the costly price be transferred to effect his ransom? How shall he wash in the fountain provided for the cleansing of every moral stain? The answer of the Gospel is—by *Faith:* "Being therefore justified by faith, we have peace with God through our Lord Jesus Christ."[141] "All that believe are justified from all things, from which ye could not be justified by the law."[142] "To him that believeth on him that justifieth the ungodly."[143]

The distinction is further made that this justification is by faith *alone*, and not by the sinner's good works: "A man is justified by faith without the deeds of the law;"[144] "Knowing that a man is not justified by the works of the law, but only through faith in Jesus Christ."[145]

This faith, generically, is in the divinity of the Lord Jesus Christ, and in the whole Gospel. But, *specifically*, it is faith in the death of Christ, in His suffering on the cross, in the offering which He made for sin. "Thus being justified freely by his grace through the redemption that is in Christ Jesus; whom God hath set forth to be a propitiation, through faith, *by his blood.*"[146] Again: "Much more then, being now justified *by his blood.*"[147]

These passages, collated, set forth the Scriptural doctrine in all its breadth, fullness and distinctness. They show that the death of Christ was vicarious; that it was the sinless One taking the place of the guilty; and that this vicarious offering is the sole ground of the sinner's justification. And they just as clearly and positively teach that the means by which the righteousness of Christ becomes the righteousness of the sinner, is faith. Not merely an intellectual conviction of the divinity of Jesus, but a heart conviction of the

---

[141] Rom. V.1.
[142] Acts Viii.39.
[143] Rom. iv.5.
[144] Rom. iii.28.
[145] Gal. ii.16.
[146] Rom. iii.24, 25.
[147] Rom. v.9.

power of His atoning death to relieve the burdened conscience. This faith is the condition of justification. The means by which the merits of Christ are appropriated. The organ by which the righteousness of Christ is transferred to the sinner.

The doctrine of Justification by Faith is thus defined by Dorner: "The free and full forgiveness of sins (effected by justification) is an objective gift,—a discovery of the gracious counsel of the love of God, who within Himself, before His inward tribunal, has for Christ's sake forgiven man,—presented to him, not because he repents and believes, but in order that he may believe...By faith man becomes *personally a partaker* of the grace of God, and, before all, of the forgiveness of sins. It is indeed an act of man, but it is an act induced or wrought by means of the love of God revealed in Christ, and of the Holy Spirit proceeding from Him."[148]

Justification is thus distinguished from sanctification in that the former is a divine act exterior to, and *for* man, whereas the latter is a divine work *in* man.

Such is the great doctrine of justification by faith, as originally proclaimed in the Gospel, and as rediscovered and republished in the Reformation. It is stated with an insistence from which there is no escape. It is God's way, and His only way, of justifying and saving the sinner.

In the face of this cumulative Scripture testimony how shall we view that tendency of so many professedly evangelical teachers to minimize faith, and to place almost the entire emphasis upon good works and life as the means of fallen man's justification before his Maker? Surely this is little less than a denial of the fundamental content of the Gospel, and a betrayal of the solemn trust to bear faithful witness to it!

When we come to examine it closely, the earnest student of God's Word, the thoughtful observer of faith, and the searcher of the deep things of the spiritual life, will find that there is a profound *rationale* in this scheme of the Gospel. Three great reasons appear why justification should be effected by faith in Christ, and by that means alone. These, as Luther saw them in his profound study and personal experience, were:

First, he who believes in Christ so clings to, rests, and reposes in Him that all Christ has becomes the soul's own, and all the soul

---

[148] History of Protestant Theology, pp. 228-230.

has—its sin and guilt—becomes Christ's. But Christ is God and man, without sin, and His righteousness and holiness are spotless and infinite. And inasmuch as He now makes the sins of the one who believes on Him His own—suffering, dying, and descending into hell for them—they are all swallowed up and effaced in Him. This is because His righteousness is stronger than all sins; His life mightier than all death; His eternal happiness more unconquerable than all evil, pain, and sorrow. And this infinite treasure now avails for the sinner. This is the supreme reason.

The second reason why faith justifies is, that when God gives His word and sends His Son as a ransom for man, nothing so honors, pleases, and glorifies Him as faith in His graciousness, whereas nothing so displeases and dishonors Him as for men to turn from Him in doubt and hardness of heart. Hence He inclines in love and mercy to the one who believes.

The third reason is that faith is the disposition that melts the heart, that powerfully moves it at the display of divine love, and hence inclines to repentance and the new life. Nothing so intensely impresses man with a conviction of his unworthiness and fills him with such a horror of sin as when he believingly sees what it has cost the Son of God. And when he beholds this unspeakable love, exercised toward him while yet in his sin and shame, he feels that he owes his life, his faculties, his all to Him who has redeemed him by such immeasurable grace. And it is in this manner that, by the energizing gift of the Holy Spirit, faith becomes the source of good works. It is the one who believes that Christ has borne the guilt and punishment of his sins, who also believes that, living or dying, he belongs, body and soul, to his Redeemer. Hence the first question of faith is: "What shall I do for Him, and how shall I actively serve Him, who has given His all for me?" Faith thus becomes the inspiration and motive power to a holy life—the root of the tree of good works—the spring and fountain of all Christian fruits and graces. Thus is faith, as the means of justification, vindicated in the philosophy of the Christian life, and in the history of Christian experience.

One of the most valuable results to be drawn from a Scriptural study and restatement of the evangelical doctrine of the Atonement will be to restore to FAITH that supreme place in the religious life which belongs to it, and from which modern thought seeks to displace it. And assuredly it is time for the disciples of faith to make a stand. Faith is a term which, in our day, we scarcely hear even mentioned in large intellectual circles. In solving our gravest problems it is to have no place.

And we cannot but observe the tendency of many orthodox Christian thinkers to yield too complacently to these illogical assumptions. Let us bear in mind, then, the paramount nature of the issue. The dearest interests of mankind are bound up with faith. If we abandon this faculty, and the spiritual sphere, the perception of which belongs to it, we surrender the last bulwark by which absolute certitude of any kind, but especially of the truths of religion, can be assured.

The Holy Scriptures are full of faith, and exalt it to the highest place, while reason is not largely dwelt upon. Faith, indeed, must be rational, but no less must reason be believing. Christianity,—the unique religion, the one ever-growing and universal religion—is built upon faith. Jesus Christ made it the corner-stone of His religious system. And all efforts by so-called progressive Christian thinkers to invert its headship for a supremacy of reason are negative and destructive.

Jesus made knowledge, salvation, and eternal life dependent upon faith; precisely the opposite of the Pagan teaching of our time, which runs: "Attend to your life, and your beliefs are a matter of indifference." Paul and the other inspired writers all developed and emphasized the same thought. And so with the Christian Fathers and great spiritual leaders of the epochal periods of Christianity. Augustine, failing with philosophy, saved the collapsing structure of ancient civilization by the Gospel of faith. Luther and his fellow-reformers, rejecting all other weapons but faith, brought about an historic revolution second only to the birth of Christianity, and opened the door for the advent of the modern age.

The triumphs of men who have prevailed by intellect and force have ended with their death, and been followed by reaction. But the great captains of faith, even from their graves, have molded the thought and life of the race, and have lived on in ever-widening circles of influence.

Let us then stand for the rights and supremacy of faith. Not alone will it solve for us the true meaning of the atonement, but it will guide us into the right interpretation and mutual relation of all the Scriptural doctrines.

And, as in the past, so in the future, will faith be the vital nerve and the conquering arm of religion. Let reason and science have their sphere in the region of nature; to faith belongs the higher realm of the spiritual, the supernatural, the invisible, and eternal. This is her legitimate sphere, and it can neither be abdicated nor transferred to another.

Let us, then, as Christians in these troubled days, when so many are asking whether the sands under their feet are shifting or no, re-light the fires of faith in God, in religion, in Holy Scripture, and in spiritual realities. Reason suffices to guide the mind of man in his narrow sail along the shore, but once out on the great ocean of truth, with every bound lost to the horizon, faith alone can take the helm and guide his frail bark until, with unerring course, it reaches the eternal haven.

CHAPTER XXV

THE MIRACLE OF THE CROSS

A MARKED characteristic of modern thought is antipathy to miracles. The disposition is to relegate the miracle to the "child age of the world." It is looked upon as belonging to the era of myth, legend and fable, when the exuberant imagination of the race had not yet been subdued by the sharp discipline of reason. Science, resting on the unbroken continuity of the order of nature and the fixed relation between cause and effect, has no place for the miracle.

Still the boast of Haeckel, that "science has traced the unbroken, causal-mechanical connection in the sphere of the natural," is repudiated by the first scientists of our times. Science, according to Du Bois Reymond, Virchow, Wundt, Lord Kelvin, and even Spencer, in his last word, has utterly failed to account for the beginnings of life, consciousness, and thought.

If then miracles must be admitted for the *origins* of physical and mental forces, why may not the divine creative might appear in miraculous form along the course of the subsequent history? Clearly, then, miracles are possible. Huxley admits their possibility, declaring the issue to be merely one of testimony. The only question is: "Has God chosen, for any purpose, to use the miracle?" Time was, when, by any who called themselves Christians, the answer to this was universally in the affirmative. The great Rationalists of the eighteenth century did not profess to receive the divine revelation. Assuming as an indisputable fact that the Bible history is interwoven with professed miracles, and that Christ claimed to perform miracles, and that the apostles fully believed this claim, and urged their evidential force for His divinity, the Rationalists, in rejecting miracles, consistently rejected the supernatural authority of the Bible and the tenets of orthodox Christianity.

But the attitude of modern so-called Christian thought is different. It is far less manly and honest, as it is far less logical. It claims to reject the miracles, but to receive the Bible. It contends that the miracles are altogether unnecessary. They have little, if any, evidential value. They are a burden to be carried, rather than an aid to faith. The best course is to dispense with them. So a Harnack, while claiming to be a foremost Christian theologian, can say: "We are fully convinced that whatever occurs in time and space is subject to the universal laws of motion, and that, therefore, in the sense of being an interruption of the continuity of nature, there can be no miracle. That a storm at sea was calmed by a single word of command, we do not believe, and never again will believe." Therefore, the Bible of Harnack is not a supernatural book; his gospel is a gospel without miracles. And he who holds with him must state, like Harnack, that Jesus does not belong to the Gospel.

We hold that this position is irrational, unscientific, and unchristian. The miracle belongs to the origin of things. The natural to its after-history. When God determined to create the world, and again to cross the bar from dead matter to life, and again to breathe into man a rational soul, He interrupted the regular order of the universe by the exercise of the miracle.

And shall we wonder, then, that when God saw the fall and ruin of the soul, the wreck of the moral universe, and determined upon its redemption, He should again call into play the miracle? The recreation demanded a no less exceptional exercise of power than did the original creation. To effect redemption there must be a break in the continuity of the moral order of the universe. There must be an incarnation. Hence there is demanded a supernatural nativity. There must be a supernatural personality—and we have the miracle of the two natures—the God-Man. The Christ must be sinless—another moral miracle. He must, too, be a miracle-worker, clothed with power over nature. And, finally, there must be the miracle of the resurrection—He must be the first one to triumph over death and break the age-long victory of the grave.

From this we see that the miracle is not a mere incident of the divine plan of redemption, to be cast aside without harm, but that it lies at the very center of the scheme, and is inseparably bound up with it. To eliminate the miraculous would tear the very heart from the revelation. The miracles prove the divinity of the Gospel, because the whole fabric of revelation is reared upon the almighty power of God intervening in the history of the race, to bring that about which to the natural order was impossible.

But the very centre of this supernatural interposition comes to pass in the atonement. That sin involves an ever-increasing servitude, an ever-tightening and unescapable chain, is the inevitable moral law. That every man shall die for his own sin is the natural order. That guilt cannot be transferred to another is a primary law of ethics. But in the death of Christ to atone for the sins of the world, in the sinless One—the All-Holy—bearing in His body and soul the guilt of the transgressors, the infinite Judge breaks in upon and suspends the universal moral order. Hence the cross becomes the miracle of miracles. The height and depth of the mystery of godliness appear in this, that "God might be just, and the justifier of him who believeth in Jesus, whom God hath set forth to be a propitiation, through faith by his blood."[149] "I do not know whether or not the universal laws of motion are thereby violated; but I do know that the greatest of miracles is here performed. An unbreakable continuity of sin held us captive, and no moral strength of ours succeeded in setting us free, but even against our will we were compelled to serve sin. Our salvation, therefore, depends on a miracle in the sense of an *interruption of the continuity of nature;* and, behold, the miracle is performed when we reach the assurance of reconciliation with God and of the forgiveness of sin at the cross of Christ. Immediately our troubled conscience is stilled, our enslaved will is liberated from the dominion of sin—the continuity of nature with respect to sin is interrupted, suspended, broken, and this is the MIRACLE OF MIRACLES."[150]

Thus does the atonement become the center of that miraculous divine power put forth to inaugurate and carry into effect the plan of redemption. And thus does the cross—that darkest scene of time—which otherwise would seem to contradict reason and justice, manifest the deepest wisdom and beneficence of Him who is at once our Creator, our Judge, and our Father.

---

[149] Rom. iii. 24, 25.

[150] Dr. S. W. Hunzinger, of Rostock, Lutheran Church Review, vol. xxii.,p. 641.

And rejoicing in the singular power of this blessed miracle of grace to heal our sore malady of sin, to bring peace to our distressed consciences and strength to our enfeebled wills, we are ready to receive all the other miracles of revelation.

The miracle of the cross is only the center and height of that series of supernatural wonders which began with the origin in time of the scheme of redemption, and whose history is recorded in the Bible.

CHAPTER XXVI

THE HOLY SPIRIT IN THE PASSION AND ATONING WORK OF CHRIST

THE third person in the Trinity—the Holy Spirit—should not be passed over in a consideration of the Scriptural doctrine of the atonement. This we are tempted to do, on account of the great prominence of the Father in the promise and covenant of grace, and of the Son—the central figure in its execution in time. But most interesting and important is the office of the Holy Spirit in this great redemptive work.

The Holy Spirit, we know, was active in the *Incarnation.* The conception of Jesus was by the agency of the Holy Ghost. And before the divine child was born, Elizabeth, on meeting His mother, Mary, was inspired of the Holy Ghost to pour forth those strains of the Magnificat which so marvelously portrayed the blessed things which the coming Savior was to confer on the race. The Holy Spirit brooded over the childhood of Jesus, and as by means of Him the child, John the Baptist, waxed strong in spirit, so, no doubt, through His influence the boy, "Jesus, increased in wisdom and stature, and in favor with God and man."[151]

The Holy Spirit had been given, in large degree, to the prophets of old, and by means of this endowment they had done mighty works, and made great revelations of truth through the gift of inspiration. But their endowment was one of limits and degrees. The supreme distinction of Christ, however, was that there was no limit to the fullness of the Spirit's indwelling in Him. "For God giveth not the Spirit by measure to him."[152] And at His baptism, when perchance the consciousness of His eternal Sonship and

---

[151] Luke ii. 52.
[152] John iii. 34.

Messianic mission was realized by Him in all its fullness, the Holy Ghost was outpoured in visible form upon His head.

We should expect, then, that when Christ came to the culminating act of His incarnation, when the supreme hour had arrived for which He had chiefly come into the world—when He was to offer Himself a ransom to redeem man from the curse, and to restore to him his forfeited heritage of eternal life—the Holy Spirit should have been an active participant.

And that such a sphere was assigned Him is shown by a remarkable passage in Hebrews. There, when the inspired writer is speaking of the cleansing power of the blood of Christ, he tells us that it was *"through the eternal Spirit* that He offered himself without spot to God."[153] While the term used is not the *Holy*, but the *Eternal* Spirit, yet we regard the view correct that "the term Eternal Spirit was chosen to indicate that the divine human person of Christ entered into such indissoluble fellowship with the Holy Spirit as even eternal death could not break...The Son was willing so to empty Himself that it would be possible for His human nature to pass through eternal death; and to this end He let it be filled with all the mightiness of the Spirit of God. Thus the Son of God offered Himself through the Eternal Spirit."[154]

If this exposition be the true one, the Holy Spirit, entering into closest fellowship with the God-Man, strengthened Him for the extreme trial, when on the cross He was to be so alienated from the Father as to be held as the representative of the guilty race, bearing in His person the righteous judgment of God upon sin.

We know that, in Gethsemane, Christ shrank from this awful ordeal, in which He should realize the pain and chill of spiritual death. And as we in our temptations, trials and crucial provings, are "strengthened with might by his Spirit in the inner man,"[155] and as we read of Christ that "in the days of his flesh, when he had offered up prayers and supplications with strong crying and tears unto Him that was able to save Him from death,"[156] so did the Holy Spirit by an angel appear to the Redeemer in the agony of His Passion in the garden, "strengthening Him" for the suffering of the

---

[153] Heb. ix. 14.
[154] Kuyper, the Holy Spirit in the Passion of Christ, pp. 104, 105.
[155] Ephes. iii. 16.
[156] Heb. v. 7.

cross, so that He could calmly say: "Nevertheless, not my will, but thine be done."[157]

The Holy Spirit, further, was the agent of the *Resurrection*, as we read: "Christ being put to death in the flesh, but quickened by the Spirit."[158] Again, Paul says that "Jesus was declared to be the Son of God by the Spirit of Holiness with power, by the resurrection from the dead."[159] He founded the Church on the day of Pentecost. He is the author of the new spiritual life of the soul in regeneration. He is the source of the efficacy of the Means of Grace.

By Him alone, therefore, it is that man, dead and impotent in trespasses and sins, is enabled to exercise that faith by which the salvation purchased by the offering of Jesus can be individually appropriated. And as we live under the dispensation of the Holy Spirit, so is He the chief agent in the economy of redemption, by which the application of its cleansing and renewing power, through all time, is made to the saved.

In the chapter, "Did God Suffer in the Atonement?" we have noted that it was the Father as well as the Son who endured sacrifice and exhibited suffering love in order to work out human redemption. And must not the same fact be predicated of the part assigned to the Holy Spirit? In His taking the place on earth vacated by the ascending Savior; in His arousing the morally burdened conscience of man to a sense of his guilt; and in striving with him to repent and be uplifted to newness of ideal and life, is there no sacrifice to be endured, no patience to be tried, no divine love to be pained? What else than this is the meaning of those passages which reprove for "doing despite to the Spirit of Grace;" for "sinning against the Holy Ghost;" for "grieving the Spirit;" and for hardening our hearts "against Him, as in the provocation and temptation of God in the wilderness?"[160]

No task is more trying, and more severely taxes every power and sympathy of our being, than the disheartenments and rebuffs encountered in trying to reclaim one who has fallen under the control of some demoralizing and disgraceful vice. And this may

---

[157] Luke xxii. 42.
[158] I Pet. iii. 18.
[159] Rom. i. 4.
[160] Heb. iii. 8.

give us a figure of what it costs "the Spirit of Holiness," the spirit of pure life and of holy and heavenly thoughts and desires, to wrestle with guilt-soiled man, to seek to raise him from the mire, and lead him, ever falling back into his old pollution, to be cleansed in the atoning blood, and to be "recreated after God in true righteousness and holiness."

But as specifically related to the passion and atoning work of Christ, the agency of the Holy Spirit was that we have stated, viz.: to strengthen Christ for the supreme moment of His great bodily and spiritual offering. Hence the work of the Holy Spirit in the scheme of redemption did not begin only at Pentecost, but the same Holy Spirit who in creation animates all life, upholds and qualifies our human nature, and through Israel and the prophets wrought the work of revelation, also prepared the body of Christ, adorned His human nature with gracious gifts, put these gifts into operation, installed Him into His office, led Him into temptation, made Him victor over the same, and finally enabled Him to finish that eternal work of satisfaction whereby our souls are redeemed.

CHAPTER XXVII

THE ATONEMENT, THE EVANGELICAL PULPIT, AND CHRISTIAN EXPERIENCE

CHRISTIANITY is the divine scheme for bringing relief to man in his dire soul distress and danger. That in it therefore which is most effective to this end will reveal its essential truth. That Christian doctrine which brings the conscience peace, which binds up the broken heart, and which heals the wounds that sin has made, will ever appeal to the believer with the most decisive power.

And this is the strongest argument for the atonement, that it has just this practical outcome. The Christian needs concern himself with no arguments or theories about it. To him it is a fact, verified in the innermost depths of his personal experience. In the offer of forgiveness through the Lamb of God who "has borne in his own body his sins on the tree," he finds the only remedy for his troubled spirit. In the love of God displayed in that suffering unto death, and in the infinite efficacy of that sacrifice, he feels that his load of guilt is removed, that his fear of judgment is gone, that he can with boldness approach God, no longer as an injured Judge, but as a loving Father, welcoming the returning prodigal as a son to His arms.

By its means he finds himself not only "reconciled to God," but led into the blessed mystical union with his suffering Savior. As Pascal beautifully says: "Jesus let only His *wounds* be touched after His resurrection. Hereby I perceive that we can now be united to Christ only through His sufferings. Yes, now, only through His atonement which these sufferings have purchased."

Hence it is the Atonement, the cross, the passion of Christ, His suffering, propiatory love, which is the chief source of evangelical power. He who would convert men, who would overcome the sinner, who would draw souls from the world to Christ, must point to the cross—must hold up the atoning death. The apostles realized this, and while they urged many other features of Christianity, yet when they would characterize the contents of their Gospel message by its chief feature, they say: "We preach Christ and Him crucified."[161] This truth has ever been the secret of the power of the Gospel. Says Amiel: "The religion of sin, of repentance and reconciliation—the religion of the new birth and the eternal life—is not a religion to be ashamed of. In spite of all the aberrations of fanaticism, all the superstitions of formalism, all the fantastic puerilities of theology, the Gospel has modified the world and consoled mankind.[162]

A Gospel devoid of atonement fails to meet human needs. Christianity without the cross is Christianity minus the Christ. It may be gratifying to intellectual pride and to the aesthetic sensibilities, but it does not satisfy the deep cravings of the religious nature. The moral theory leaves the deepest longings of the sin-smitten soul unsatisfied. Not a "white marble Christ," but a suffering Savior is the one that moves and saves. "I, if I be lifted up from the earth, will draw all men unto me."[163] "Christ," says Jean Paul Richter, "with His pierced hands, lifted the gates of empires from their hinges and changed the currents of history."

The lack of this doctrine will enervate any pretended Christian scheme. The rationalist Bauer, in the time when unbelief filled the theological chairs, complained that you had but to mention to the multitude the name of Jesus and hold up the cross, and all the learned doubts of great critical masters proved ineffectual and vain. Horace Bushnell, some time after announcing his subjective theory of the atonement,—denying a true satisfaction, and making the cross little else than a power of influence and example,—admitted that "his system utterly lacked efficiency unless clothed in the altar-terms which belong to the orthodox system." And Kuenen, a foremost representative of the radical higher criticism, lately complained that "no student could procure a congregation if it were known that he had graduated at the theological seminary where these views were taught." Those who are seeking the bread

---

[161] I Cor. ii. 2.
[162] Journal Intime, p. 140.
[163] John xii. 32.

of life for their spiritual needs and comfort for their troubled consciences, know too well that they cannot be fed upon ethical husks.

So this truth has ever lain at the root of all spiritual power, of all successful work for the cause of religion. The doctrine of a vicarious atonement for the sins of men has been in all history the most intense incentive to evangelizing effort. It has made the missionary and the martyr. It has been the unvarying impulse to the most self-denying labors in behalf of others. It has always begotten a spirit of self-sacrifice in those who have believed it.

"By their fruits shall ye know them."[164] Every other idea of atonement has resulted in a paralysis of earnest and persistent effort toward the evangelization of the world. Neither missionary nor martyr are its fruits. It has no victorious power. The great doctrine of the atonement needs peculiarly to be studied in the light of its triumphant achievement and its rare fruitage. The world may have advanced wonderfully in scientific achievement, in learning, and in material arts, but never can it safely get away from the cross. That would be no progress, but a retrogression to the dark ages. Never, while sin and conscience and death last, will the great redeeming sacrifice lose its power. The experience of mankind will ever cling to it as the hope and anchor of the sin-burdened, storm-tossed spirit, and as the fructifying seed of spiritual life.

There is too much reason to fear that in our time many pulpits are getting away from the simplicity of the Gospel. The literary, the historical, the critical, or ethical element predominates over the doctrines of sin and grace. There must be a return of emphasis on the old truths that have always been the mighty ones in raising men out of the death in trespasses and sins, and rousing the Church to a deeper sense of responsibility for a world lying in wickedness. The doctrines of sin, atonement, retribution, and justification by faith—as the God-appointed way of salvation—must be preached if men are to be convicted, converted, and saved.

These doctrines are the levers to lift the world and the Church toward God. Of Charles G. Finney it was said, his power to reach men—leading men, professional men, physicians, lawyers, teachers—has seldom been equaled; and in reaching them he

---

[164] Matt. vii. 20.

preached wrath and condemnation on the one side, and a free and full justification by faith on the other side. It was this kind of preaching with which Luther shook the world, and which has been the source of power in all the great preachers who have ever lived.

It was the lack of the atonement in his conviction and public speech which made Henry Ward Beecher, with all his genius and accomplishments, simply the greatest of platform lecturers, while it was insistence on this heart of the Gospel which made Spurgeon, with his limited original endowment and want of oratorical graces, still the greatest preacher of modern times.

This is the Gospel adapted alike to the ignorant and the learned Christian, for it is adapted to that spiritual experience which is common to every sin-burdened soul. The Christian knows it to be the very essence of the Gospel, for it has approved itself to his needs with a power that nothing else can bring. It has justified itself to the inmost depths of his soul. Living or dying, in joy or in sorrow, in light and in darkness, it is his strength, his solace, his guide and his hope. Trusting in a crucified Savior alone, he can win his moral fight, conquer every doubt, quiet every sting of conscience, overcome the fear of death, and enter into life. His humble yet confident cry is:

> Nothing in my hand I bring,
> Simply to Thy cross I cling;
> Naked, come to Thee for dress;
> Helpless, look to Thee for grace;
> Foul, I to the Fountain fly,
> Wash me, Savior, or I die.

CHAPTER XXVIII

THE ATONEMENT IN THE ETERNITIES—PAST AND TO COME

So pre-eminent was the redemptive work of Christ that it was by no means confined to time. It touched the two eternities—that past and that to come. Its root was in the one, its flower in the other. Time was but the drama of its execution. Its purpose was conceived in the eternity of old, and its blissful fruition is attained in heaven.

Peter, in his sermon on the day of Pentecost, made the declaration: "Jesus of Nazareth, being delivered by the determinate counsel and foreknowledge of God, ye have taken, and by wicked hands have crucified and slain."[165] Here we learn that the crucifixion was a definite part of the divine purpose. Christ was "delivered" to the cross "by the determinate counsel and foreknowledge of God." In the Epistles of Peter this eternal decree is shown to extend to the purifying power of the suffering sacrifice, thus, "Elect, according to the foreknowledge of God the Father through the sprinkling of the blood of Jesus Christ."[166]

On this striking passage Alford comments: "It is in the mind of the apostle that the death of Christ is not only, as *looking back on the past*, a propitiation for sin, thereby removing the obstacle which stood in the way of God's gracious purpose toward man— but also, as *looking forward to the future*, a capacitating of us for the participation in God's salvation."[167] In Peter we are further told when in the past eternity this divine decree originated. For when there it is asserted that we are "redeemed not with corruptible things, but with the precious blood of Christ," the apostle adds the

---

[165] Acts ii.23.
[166] I Pet. i.2.
[167] Greek Testament, vol. iv., p. 332.

important statement revealed to him by inspiration of the Holy Ghost: "Who verily was *foreordained* indeed *before the foundation of the world*, but was manifest in these last times for you."[168] Here the declaration is made that before the foundation stone of the creation was laid, it had been ordained that the precious blood of atonement should be shed.

The brilliant French preacher, Masillon, in one of his eloquent and thoughtful sermons, says: "If someone would have told us beforehand that God would create a world wherein would come to pass sin, and sorrow, and misery and death, and all the wrongs, heartaches and tragedies of time, we would have said, 'That would be impossible to a being of infinite goodness and love. But now that we see such a creation as an actual fact, we learn that it was possible.'"[169] And so with many other facts, mysteries to us, but clear to the divine wisdom and holiness.

But in this eternal decree for human redemption we doubtless see an explanation of one of these greatest apparent inconsistencies. When God conceived the glorious thought of the creation of man, made in His image by the moral faculty and by the prerogative of free-will, He foresaw the fall and all its fateful issues. And to counteract these, He, at once, coeval with the creative concept, decreed the sending of His Son, and permitted the dark acts of His passion, that, by this mysterious means, not only should the dire evils of sin and death be counteracted, but overruled to the highest good of the creature and to the brightest glory of the Creator. And what a lesson do we not learn, from this revelation, of faith and reverence toward Him with "whom there is the hiding of power," and of whom the Psalmist in adoring humility says: "Thy way is in the sea, and thy path in the great waters, and thy footsteps are not known."[170]

The wondrous revelation does not, however, by any means end here. That scheme which occupied the divine thought in the councils of ancient eternity, and which had its fulfillment in time, is carried over in scene and blessed effect to the eternity to come. As Moses and Elijah conversed with the Lord on the Mount of Transfiguration respecting the holy wonders of His decease, and

---

[168] I Peter i. 20.

[169] Sermons, vol. ii., p. 319.

[170] Ps. lxxvii. 19.

as "the angels desire to look into" "the sufferings of Christ and the glory that should follow,"[171] so will the future world unveil many of the now hidden mysteries of redemptive grace. For here we but "see through a glass darkly, but then face to face."[172] As

> On earth the broken arcs;
> In heaven the perfect round,

so will the eternity to come reveal the glory of the cross as it cannot now be conceived.

Foregleams of this are cast in the Scriptures. In the visions of the Apocalypse "the Lamb slain from the foundation of the world"[173] is a frequent figure. The explanation of this symbol is no doubt to be found in the fact that as Jesus, when He appeared in His resurrection body, bore the wounds of His crucifixion, so He ascended bearing these redemptive marks to His heavenly state as the glorified Son of man, to wear them as signs of honor throughout eternity.

When, therefore, the redeemed saints behold their Lord in His divine majesty, yet marked by the traces of the love that purchased their souls with His blood, He fulfills to their adoring gaze the type of the Lamb of God slain for the sin of the world. And so the highest point in the visions of the Apocalypse, and the climax of the rapturous worship of heaven, is reached when the "four living ones and the twenty elders fall down before the Lamb," and all the saints join their prayers, and "They sing a new song, saying, Thou art worthy, for thou wast slain, and hast redeemed us to God by thy blood out of every kindred, and tongue, and people, and nation."[174]

The atonement then stretches over two eternities. That which God conceived before time began shall not disappear when time shall be no more. The crowning work of the highest attribute of divinity—love—shall never be erased from the records of eternity. Never shall the saints forget the precious blood by which they were redeemed. Never shall the note of gratitude to the slain Lamb, foreordained from before the foundation of the world, cease to inspire the deepest theme of their praise, as they stand on the sea

---

[171] I Peter i.11, 12.

[172] I Cor. xiii. 12.

[173] Rev. xiii. 8 and xvii. 8.

[174] Rev. v.9.

of glass before the throne, bearing the harps of God, and sing the old, but ever new song of redemption.

CHAPTER XXIX

CONCLUSION

THE atonement is the most precious, blood-red jewel sparkling in the coronet of the Christian faith. It is dear to the heart, because it speaks the infinite worth and power of a Savior to ransom from the nameless evil of sin. It is precious, because it reveals the measureless depth and height of that divine love which could undergo so mighty a sacrifice for the redemption of the lost creature. "The Atonement," says Fairbairn, "in the degree that it exhibits God as a being who does not need to be moved to mercy, but who suffers unto sacrifice that He may save, exalts in the eyes of all created intelligences His character and mercy."[175] It is vital, moreover, because it is that one supreme motive which awakens the sleeping conscience, and which, through the agency of the Holy Spirit, in the new birth of love, becomes the source of that spiritual life to which the Church owes all her evangelical ardor, missionary zeal, and passionate fire for souls.

Hence the purpose of this volume is to enforce the duty of fidelity to this fundamental doctrine, and the urgent need of its positive presentation. Let us never imagine that we can strengthen Christianity by leaving out the great doctrines which have given it joy and power. Faith is not the mere indulgence of the emotions. It is the acceptance of truth,—positive, unchanging, revealed truth,—in regard to God and the world, Christ and the soul, duty and immortality. The human spirit still thirsts for God. Men will not be drawn to Christianity by ethical addresses, or appeals to sociability and brotherhood, or by vague and misty human opinions. They hunger for the divine. They want to hear religion. They yearn for the eternal and invisible. Their guilt cries out for a divine and all-

---

[175] The Atonement, p. 487.

potent Savior. The finite in them calls for the infinite. The creature spirit feels a void which none but its Creator can fill. The human can find rest alone in God—the sum of all being, perfection and power. What is required is to give strong and sturdy reaffirmation to the really great themes of our holy religion.

The mission of every Christian, then, high or low, is to bear testimony to this great evangelical doctrine, and to hold it up inviolate, as the saving need of every age, and especially of our own. And that much is being done in our day to weaken its import, and to render men more or less indifferent to it, who can fail to see?

In a late issue of the *North American Review*, commenting upon the indiscriminate praise heaped upon Emerson by many representative American thinkers at the recent centennial of his birth, the remark is made: "It must be admitted that Emerson deliberately shunned the darker aspects of life. He did not face the problem of sin. Christians may still claim that theirs is the only religion that has effectually measured its strength with sin, sorrow and death."[176] It does this, by means of the atonement, and the love which this surpassing divine love unto sacrifice awakens. The soul, relieved of its intolerable burden, is uplifted and inspired with new spiritual life and power, by the same love which has redeemed it.

To surrender, compromise, or in any degree impair its confession of the atonement, is for Christianity to abnegate its life. The struggle is one touching its very essence. This the opponents of Christianity, whether open or hidden, whether claiming to be foe or friend, well understand. Hence it is this central, evangelical doctrine which evokes the deadliest fire. It is still, as of old, the offense of the cross. Natural reason, human pride, the worldly spirit, will have none of a vicarious redemption.

Let us not think it strange, then, that every artifice and resource of opposition should seek to subvert this very citadel of our evangelical confession. And let Christendom everywhere stand for it with columns unwavering and undaunted. Never has the Church universal been willing to waive a jot or tittle of this her cardinal belief. And Christ the Rock, immovable by all the powers of darkness, underlies His church today just as in all the ages of the past.

---

[176] Vol. 176, p. 685.

Deceived and misled, then, by none, let every Christian bow before the cross, and adore the Son of God suffering for the sake of the world, proclaim His blood as the only ransom for sin to fallen and lost souls, and, by faith in His all-availing sacrifice, conquer all the forces of unbelief, overcome death, and gain the life eternal.

> Jesus, all our thoughts excelling,
> For Thy love and grief a dwelling
> Pure and holy make in me;
> > Let me know Thy crucifying;
> > Let me feel the pains of dying
> Thou didst suffer on the tree.
>
> Let my heart with Thine be riven;
> Let Thy cup to me be given;
> Let me of its depths partake;
> > And still flaming thus with fervor
> > Let me find Thee my Preserver,
> When the Judgment Day shall break.
>
> Through Thy cross redemption send me;
> Let Thy death from sin defend me;
> Save me by Thy tender love.
> > When this mortal flesh shall perish,
> > Evermore my spirit cherish
> In Thy Paradise above.
> —*Stabat Mater Dolorosa* (Thirteenth Century).